The Rondine Method

The Rondine Method

A Relational Approach to Conflict

EDITED BY
FRANCO VACCARI
MIGUEL H. DÍAZ
CHARLES HAUSS

ROWMAN & LITTLEFIELD
Lanham • Boulder • New York • London

Executive Acquisitions Editor: Michael Kerns
Assistant Editor: Elizabeth Von Buhr
Sales and Marketing Inquiries: textbooks@rowman.com

Credits and acknowledgments for material borrowed from other sources, and reproduced with permission, appear on the appropriate pages within the text.

Published by Rowman & Littlefield
An imprint of The Rowman & Littlefield Publishing Group, Inc.
4501 Forbes Boulevard, Suite 200, Lanham, Maryland 20706
www.rowman.com

86-90 Paul Street, London EC2A 4NE

British Library Cataloguing in Publication Information Available

Library of Congress Cataloging-in-Publication Data

Names: Vaccari, Franco, 1952- editor. | Díaz, Miguel H., editor. | Hauss, Charles, editor.
Title: The Rondine method : a relational approach to conflict / edited by Franco Vaccari, Miguel H. Diaz, Charles Hauss.
Description: Lanham, Maryland : Rowman & Littlefield, 2023. | Series: Peace and security in the 21st century | Includes bibliographical references and index.
Identifiers: LCCN 2022055816 (print) | LCCN 2022055817 (ebook) | ISBN 9781538177167 (cloth) | ISBN 9781538177174 (paperback) | ISBN 9781538177181 (ebook)
Subjects: LCSH: Peace-building—Psychological aspects. | Peace-building—Social aspects. | Youth in peace-building. | Interpersonal relationships. | Religions—Relations. | Cultural relations. | Rondine Cittadella della Pace.
Classification: LCC JZ5538 .R66 2023 (print) | LCC JZ5538 (ebook) | DDC 327.1/72—dc23/eng/20230105
LC record available at https://lccn.loc.gov/2022055816
LC ebook record available at https://lccn.loc.gov/2022055817

To Rondine's students—past, present, and future

About the Peace and Security in the 21st Century Series

Until recently, security was defined mostly in geopolitical terms with the assumption that it could only be achieved through at least the threat of military force. Today, however, people from as different backgrounds as planners in the Pentagon and veteran peace activists think in terms of human or global security, where no one is secure unless everyone is secure in all areas of their lives. This means that it is impossible nowadays to separate issues of war and peace, the environment, sustainability, identity, global health, and the like.

The books in the series aim to make sense of this changing world of peace and security by investigating security issues and peace efforts that involve cooperation at several levels. By looking at how security and peace interrelate at various stages of conflict, the series explores new ideas for a fast-changing world and seeks to redefine and rethink what peace and security mean in the first decades of the new century.

Multidisciplinary in approach and authorship, the books cover a variety of topics, focusing on the overarching theme that students, scholars, practitioners, and policymakers must find new models and theories to account for, diagnose, and respond to the difficulties of a more complex world. Authors are established scholars and practitioners in their fields of expertise.

In addition, it is hoped that the series will contribute to bringing together authors and readers in concrete, applied projects, and thus help create, under the sponsorship of Alliance for Peacebuilding (AfP), a community of practice.

The series is sponsored by the Alliance for Peacebuilding (http://www.all ianceforpeacebuilding.org/) and edited by Charles Hauss, senior fellow for innovation and emeritus member, Board of Directors.

Contents

Acknowledgments   xi

Foreword: Address of His Holiness Pope Francis to the Rondine
Association Vatican, December 3, 2018   xv
   Pope Francis

Introduction: On the Love of God and Our Enemies: Hospitality
and the Rondine Method   1
   Miguel H. Díaz

PART 1: THE RONDINE METHOD *FRANCO VACCARI*   **9**

1   The Steps toward Trust   11
   Franco Vaccari

2   The Other Person in the Relationship   27
   Franco Vaccari

3   The Heart of the Rondine Method: The Relational
   Approach to Conflict   37
   Franco Vaccari

4   Putting the Relational Model to the Test   51
   Franco Vaccari

5   Some Final Thoughts and Next Steps   67
   Franco Vaccari

PART 2: RESPONSES TO THE RONDINE METHOD   77

6   Rondine Cittadella Della Pace: An Open-Air Laboratory
    about Intergroup Conflict and Intergroup Contact Theory   79
    Ariela Pagani, Anna Bertoni, A. Garuglieri, and Raffaella Iafrate

7   The Rondine Method and Foreign Policy   97
    Michael David Kaiser

8   The Rondine Method and Creative Conflict Transformation:
    Insights from Contact Theory and Interreligious Peacebuilding 103
    Gerard Powers

9   The Rondine Method: Building Peace through Compassion   113
    Daniel Rothbart and Susan Allen

Conclusion: Today Rondine, Tomorrow the World   129
    Charles Hauss

Bibliography   139

Index   147

About the Contributors   153

Acknowledgments

This book has been a labor of love in every sense of the term. For Franco, that love goes back to long before Rondine itself was created, when the village was in ruins and the idea of a *Cittadella della Pace* was little more than a dream. For Miguel and Chip, the labor of love began later when Miguel found out about Rondine while he was serving as U.S. Ambassador to the Holy See from 2009 to 2012 and when Chip was asked to speak at a Rondine event in 2018.

Together, we would like to start by thanking the students who have made Rondine what it is, its staff, and its many supporters around the world.

From Franco:

The publication of this volume in English takes place thanks to a rich series of generous and qualified donations and to numerous generous collaborations. The first thanks go to the former ambassador of Italy to the United States, Armando Varricchio, who wanted the presentation and the first public discussion on the Rondine Method to take place in the Italian embassy in Washington, DC, giving the initiative undisputed prestige and success. This event on December 12, 2018, was specifically valuable at a time when we took the first steps to make the Rondine Method known in the United States.

At that event in Washington, we arrived with the first studies on the method published in Italy. Unfortunately, not all the researchers were able to join the Washington event, but Raffaella Iafrate and Anna Bertoni, psychologists, colleagues, and professors at the Catholic University of the Sacred Heart in Milan served as surrogate voices who spoke on behalf of other friends, especially the psychologist colleagues of Rondine Academy: Claudia Bernardini, Francesca Nofri, and Teresa Fantacchiotti. To them—and through them, to the others—my gratitude.

Also on that occasion, I came up with the first Italian–English bilingual text, *Rondine Method*. Although provisional since it was written at a pace dictated by urgency, I am indebted to my brotherly friend Giordano Remondi for that very useful effort. Remondi is an interdisciplinary researcher and co-author with Nunzio Galantino of the last book published in September 2022 by the Il Mulino Publishing Company, *The Odd Couple: Relationship and Conflict. On the Route of the Rondine Method.*

When first steps are taken in a method that addresses conflict transformation, it is natural to expect considerable interest to arise and some irrepressible fear. The latter can only be soothed by an authoritative reception of this method. This is why my most sincere gratitude goes to the Italian and American authors who have produced their contributions in this volume, who have hosted me at their universities allowing me to lecture on the Rondine Method, and who have studied or even, as in the case of Daniel Rothbart and Susan Allen, set up an experimental research project on the method.

The first of the final two words of gratitude is to Miguel Díaz and Charles "Chip" Hauss. This English-language book exists thanks to them. The reader will be able to approach the text in an authentic and faithful way thanks to the refined translation work done by Miguel Díaz as a result of the time he spent in conversation and consultation with me and my staff. A process was led by Spinella Dell'Avanzato and Mauro D'Andrea to update and nuance the linguistic terms and conceptual arguments. The process is in the course of codification, and above all, the translation responds to an attempt to authentically diffuse the content of the method in linguistic and cultural contexts different from the one in which it was born.

The second thanks goes—as always and above all—to all those coupled "enemies," these future leaders from countries at war who have courageously accepted the invitation to pursue the two-year program of the World House proposed by Rondine. Without them, the Rondine Method would never have been born. Together with them, I dedicate this common effort to the young people of the world who desire to reject the logic that creates enemies and set aside the reality of wars.

From Miguel:

I could not have contributed to this project without the life-giving relations and conversations that I have cultivated over the years with the international students and leaders of this transformative peacebuilding program. At Rondine Cittadella della Pace, I have discovered practical, experiential, and well-reasoned approaches that promote bridge-building among diverse peoples and speak to the cornerstone principle of religious traditions, namely, the love of one's neighbor. I am grateful to be included in Rondine's unwavering vision to overcome conflict and send forth students as ambassadors who labor in our world to turn strangers into friends. Finally, I want to thank my graduate assistant Mr. Zaccary Haney for his support in helping us proofread this book.

From Chip:

I owe much to my colleagues at the Alliance for Peacebuilding who could not get to a meeting organized by Rondine in 2019 and sent me instead; Gretchen Sandles, who accompanied me on my trip to Rondine and on my trip through life; and all the people in my networks who have helped shape my views about personal growth, social change, peacebuilding, and more.

Finally, we all want to thank the team at Rowman & Littlefield. Erin Cler did a great job of copy editing a book whose contributors wrote using a wide variety of styles. Elizabeth Von Buhr and Crystal Branson shepherded this book through the production process. Most of all, we should thank our acquisitions editor twice. Not only did Michael Kerns agree to take on this project, but he bailed Chip out early in the editing process by introducing him to some wonderful technology-driven online summer camps that his grandson could attend and thus give him more time to focus on this project when it needed it most.

Foreword

ADDRESS OF HIS HOLINESS POPE FRANCIS TO THE RONDINE ASSOCIATION VATICAN, DECEMBER 3, 2018[1]

Pope Francis

Dear brothers and sisters, I welcome you with joy on the twentieth anniversary of the "Rondine-Cittadella della Pace" Association. I greet the president, Mr. Franco Vaccari, and I thank him for his introduction. I greet Cardinal Gualtiero Bassetti, who from the beginning has supported this entity, noting in it the "perfume" of the venerable Giorgio La Pira, and the archbishop of Arezzo-Cortona-Sansepolcro, Riccardo Fontana. In a special way I greet you, young people, who come from countries which are theatres of conflict that have degenerated into various forms of violence and war, and who live in Rondine, the experience of the international student body. And you, young people from all the Italian regions, with your teachers in the fourth year of high school. And you too, former students, members, supporters and friends. Welcome!

Your educational commitment is to host young people who, in various parts of the world, live stranded in cultures poisoned by pain and hatred, and to offer them a bold challenge: to verify in person whether the other, he or she who is beyond a closed boundary, of barbed wires or impassable walls, is really what everyone claims: an enemy. In these twenty years you have developed a method capable of transforming conflicts, of bringing young people out of this deception and restoring them to their peoples for a full spiritual, moral, cultural and civil development: generous young people who, innocent, are born with the burden of the failures of previous generations.

You have founded this work on two great spiritual roots of your land: Saint Francis of Assisi, who received the stigmata in La Verna, and Saint Romualdo, founder of Camaldoli. You have chosen well!

I, too, when I chose the name of Francis, thought of the poor and of peace. Poverty—in the negative sense—and war are linked in a vicious circle that kills people, fuels untold suffering and spreads a hatred that never ends. By choosing to dedicate yourselves to young people, you also commit yourselves to fighting poverty and building peace, as a work of justice and love. An action that nourishes hope and places trust in man, especially in young people.

La Pira wrote that La Verna is "the launch pad for enterprises of peace." On that mountain there is a mystery of pain and transfiguring love and you, who have developed the Rondine Method for the creative transformation of conflicts, up there you receive continuous inspiration to progress in the service of the common good. And so you have the privilege of gathering buds for a flowering of peace for all of humanity.

I have listened to the appeal that you have written and which you will present at the UN on 10 December, on the occasion of the seventieth anniversary of the Universal Declaration of Human Rights. Listening to a young Palestinian and a young Israeli who together ask the governments of the world to take a step that can reopen the future, transferring the cost of a weapon from the defense budget to the education budget to form a peace leader, is a rare thing, it is a bright thing! How could you disagree? But we adults cannot get away saying "Well done!" No. I feel I have to give you all my support, my sympathy, my blessing.

Indeed, your appeal contains and proposes a concrete vision. In the Message for the next World Day of Peace, on 1 January 2019, which has as its theme *Good politics is at the service of peace*, I reiterate that political responsibility belongs to every citizen, in particular to those who have received the mandate to protect and to rule. This mission consists in safeguarding the law and encouraging dialogue between the actors of society, between generations and between cultures. Listening to you, I add: between the parties in conflict. Because trust is created only in dialogue.

When the human being is respected in his fundamental rights—as Saint John XXIII recalled in his Encyclical Pacem in Terris (1963)—the sense of the duty to respect the rights of others arises in him. Rights and duties increase the awareness of belonging to the same community, with others and with God (cf. ibid., 45). We are therefore called to bring and announce peace as the good news of a future where every living being will be considered in his dignity and his rights.

You, dear young people, have chosen to meet when everything around you and inside you said: but why? What is it for? Will it be right? And, after the two years of formation at Rondine, you have overturned your feelings, your thoughts, you have brought about mutual trust and now you are ready to take on professional, civil and political responsibilities for the good of your peoples. You are already those young leaders who in the appeal you ask States and peoples to commit themselves to forming together!

You ask us to join your appeal. For my part, I will do so, and I ask the Heads of State and Government to do the same. Your voice—weak, but strong in the hope and courage of youth—can be heard on 10 December at the United Nations. There is a need for leaders with a new mentality. Those who do not know how to dialogue and exchange with each other are not leaders of peace: a leader who does not try to meet the "enemy," to sit with him at the table as you do, cannot lead his people to peace. To do this we need humility, not arrogance: Saint Francis helps you to follow this path with courage. Listening to young people, even in the recent Synod in which they were protagonists, I learned a lot from them. I hope your leaders come to Rondine and see how their young people are preparing peace.

I rejoice that you have chosen the Encyclical *Laudato si'* as a fundamental text for your school: indeed, integral ecology offers the prospect for humanity to conceive of itself as one family and to consider the Earth as a common home. It is good that with your method you want to reach citizens and political leaders, representatives of national and international institutions at the same time. Indeed, peace is the responsibility of every person. This is why, together with the Cardinal Secretary of State, you have met the Diplomatic Corps at the Holy See. With the efforts of everyone, we must definitively remove war from the planet and from the history of humanity.

Dear friends, may this twenty-year anniversary of your Association renew the momentum for spreading your simple and strong testimony, your method, your desire for change in the world, which, starting from relationships, pervades every aspect of life. May you help break down the highest walls, build bridges and eliminate impassable borders, the legacy of a world that is ending. You have overcome the hardest barriers, those within each of you, dissolving the deception of the enemy, and you have surprised yourselves by re-opening boundaries blocked by wars. Please never lose your wonder and humility. Dear young people of Rondine, safeguard the trust you have gained among you and transform it into a generous task of service to the common good. Mr. President, may the work you have initiated continue! For this I bless all of you, from my heart, and your loved ones, and I assure you of my prayer. You too, please, remember to pray for me. Thank you.

Note

1. Speech delivered by Pope Francis to Rondine Cittadella della Pace on December 3, 2018, before representatives from Rondine traveled to the UN in New York. At the UN, they launched the "Leaders for Peace" global campaign. Afterward, they traveled to Washington, DC, for an event hosted by the Italian embassy on the Rondine Method. Reprinted from https://press.vatican.va/content/salastampa/en/bollettino/pubblico/2018 /12/03/181203g.html.

Introduction

ON THE LOVE OF GOD AND OUR ENEMIES: HOSPITALITY AND THE RONDINE METHOD

Miguel H. Díaz

Figure 0.1.   Holy Trinity, Andrej Rublev, 1425-1427 **Source:** Wikimedia

The best word to describe the inspiration behind the Metodo Rondine is still the same one first used by the pioneers in 1997: hospitality. An archetypal concept, that will always live in human beings when these are *resilient* people: they "bend" when conflict degenerates into the destructive violence of war, but they do not "break." The host stubbornly seeks with passion and rationality to find new balance and harmony.

—Franco Vaccari, *Metodo Rondine*

The most famous fifteenth-century icon of the Trinity was inspired by the familial hospitality that the biblical patriarch Abraham and his wife Sarah offered to three migrating strangers who arrived at their home. Its artist, Andrei Rublev, links this central biblical story in Genesis 18 to capture the heart of the Christian doctrine of God. In Christian theology, God is love, inclusion, and hospitality. Christians believe that in Jesus, God has reached out to welcome humanity and in this act of extravagant and life-giving hospitality, became flesh. Rublev depicts this hospitable nature of God by positioning three angels sitting around a common table in an open circle. Their bodies turned toward one another invite us to consider that human persons created in the divine image are called to exist in communal dialogue and openness to one another. The God that Rublev iconically captures is a God who calls us from isolation into relationship. In God's image, humans are called to turn to one another daily in acts of hospitality and in ordinary household settings. We discover our common humanity when we welcome one another in conversation, transformational personal encounters, and the sharing of life-sustaining resources.

Rublev's icon captures a central biblical motif and ethical cornerstone connected to divine agency and desire. God calls Israel to welcome the stranger (Hebrew, תושב גר:ger, "foreigner," "stranger," "alien"). God calls Israel and its descendants to practice hospitality for the sake of those who have often been exiled from community and life-giving relationships. Just like God welcomed Israel during its time of exile and estrangement in the land of Egypt, the people of Israel must do the same when it comes to receiving foreigners, strangers, and estranged people in their midst (Deuteronomy 10:19). God reminds Israel that by listening to and welcoming these "exiles," it will welcome God's messengers without knowing it, as many have: "Do not forget to show hospitality to strangers, for by so doing some people have shown hospitality to angels without knowing it" (Hebrews 13:1-2).

The hospitality of Abraham and Sarah offers a window into human actions that pave the way to (re)discover our common humanity. The challenge of practicing hospitality may come easy for those with whom we share similar values; less so when we face those who are different from us; those who exist outside our relational cultural, religious, and political circles; and those we might even consider threats to our existence. But this biblical story of hospitality captures what rabbi Jonathan Sacks has characterized as the most basic ethical commandment of the Bible. "Nowhere is the singularity of ethics more evident," affirms Sacks, "than in its treatment of the issue that has proved to be most difficult in the history of human interaction, namely *the problem of the stranger*, the one who is not like us," for as he underscores with respect to rabbinic commentary, "the Hebrew Bible in one verse commands, 'You shall love your neighbour as yourself', but in no fewer than 36 places commands us to 'love the stranger'" (Sacks 2002, 58).

This book offers an introduction to the *Rondine Method*, a method that in the words of Franco Vaccari, founder and president of Rondine Cittadella della Pace Association, can be summed up by one simple word: *hospitality*. The Rondine Method translates the biblical commandment to love strangers as a daily and household practice that invites international students to face, encounter, and love those perceived as enemies. Rondine challenges these students to set aside prejudices and life-threatening social constructions of the self. In this two-year process of "*convivenza*" at Rondine, of living together and interpersonal sharing, so-called enemies become lifelong friends. Upon completion of the program, these students, transformed by the practice of hospitality, return to their countries of origin as ambassadors of peace. Indeed, "A living-together (*convivenza*) that creates the safe space to befriend persons once considered enemies, enables the youth of Rondine to overcome human differences and life-threatening divisions" (Díaz 2019).

I was first introduced to the Rondine Method during my diplomatic service as the U.S. ambassador to the Holy See (2009–2012). Since then, I have remained committed to its educational vision of addressing conflict and continue to be a strong advocate of what Rondine calls "popular diplomacy." Like the hospitality of Abraham and Sarah, the Rondine Method encourages estranged students to face one another around common tables in a familial setting. The Rondine Method prepares students to become ambassadors of peace, carrying the bridge-building skills they have learned with them back to the various places they come from where violence and war often rule the day. Like the ordinary and transformative hospitality that the patriarch and matriarch offered to three strangers, Rondine's youth-led diplomacy welcomes strangers to a familial setting in a citadel tucked away in Tuscany. From this Tuscan village, human transformation moves into other lands, the places where Rondine sends off its newly constituted ambassadors to embody peace and almost certainly, amidst conflict, violence, war, and division.

The Rondine Method and Its Reception

In his address to Rondine students on December 3, 2018, at the Vatican, which also starts this book, Pope Francis underscored that "only through dialogue can trust be created." At Rondine, dialogue opens up spaces that enable students who once perceived themselves as enemies to begin a process of encountering and rediscovering their common humanity. Leaving behind their war- and conflict-torn lands, familial and familiar spaces, the students who come to Rondine take the courageous step to live together (*convivenza*), learn a new common language (Italian), and take great risks as they become transparent and vulnerable with each other. Yet as Vaccari observes in this book, "Slowly but surely, youthful former enemies come to understand that conflict can be a good thing by learning how to identify and accept the similarities and differences that grow out of the kinds of frictions" (2018a).

As I see it, Rondine's success lies in creating a transformative and relational process that encourages the deconstruction of life-threatening perceptions and ideologies associated with the communities that have shaped them. Tearing down these relational walls and building bridges of understanding is not easy, but it is essential to birthing new and more inclusive ways of relating and encountering our common humanity. At Rondine, students create relational safe spaces by living with their so-called enemies, interacting daily with them and joining arms with them to tear down the cultural, political, religious, and other humanly constructed barriers that have kept them apart. The Rondine Method is not a theory-driven exercise intended to *produce* certain ends in addressing conflict and building peace, however noble these results may be. The Rondine Method can best be understood as *praxis* in the Aristotelian sense of the term. The Rondine Method invites us to consider that the practice of hospitality has value in and of itself; it is a "human activity whose end is internal to, rather than external to, itself" (Goizueta 1995, 82).[1] In other words, the Rondine Method encourages us to practice hospitality because facing and welcoming others and their distinct differences is itself a valuable and self-transformative action. Living hospitality, becoming creatures of hospitality, *is* what enables us to embrace others in the solidarity of our common humanity. In this sense, the Rondine Method is not just about fostering valuable skills and peacebuilding practices, although there is plenty of wisdom that the method offers. It is more about becoming humanly transformed by our encounter with others and their distinct differences.

In the first five chapters of this book, Vaccari explores distinct features of the Rondine Method. Chapter 1, "The Steps toward Trust," discusses the initial steps that students take as they commit to the two-year process to accompany one another. As they undertake this process, the Rondine Method invites students to critically examine prejudices and social presuppositions that have shaped their humanity. Students begin to embrace relationship and solidarity with one another. They take baby steps that eventually lead to trusting even those once considered their enemies. Slowly, they grow in wisdom from this daily accompaniment as they increasingly welcome conflict without fearing communal violence and division.

Chapter 2, "The Other Person in the Relationship," reflects on this holistic approach. This approach, while highly existential, draws from psychopedagogical research tested over the twenty years that this program has existed. In this chapter, Vaccari begins to mine the relationship between the individual and the community, underscoring the communal constitution of the self and the traumatic experiences that haunt people as a result of past traumas. These traumatic experiences, or "relational shocks," as he characterizes them, become ghostlike memories that often trigger relational tensions among the students. The Rondine Method encourages students to embrace these tensions as an opportunity for self-healing regarding perceived and internalized personal threats.

Chapter 3 continues to develop "The Heart of the Rondine Method: The Relational Approach to Conflict." Drawing on the scholarship of philosophers; sociologists; and especially, psychologists, he underscores the notion of the self as relational, communal, and social. The Rondine Method highlights the capacity of the human imagination to create and envision new possibilities for establishing collaborative relationships from the existing inimical interactions that students embody when they first arrive. This is an essential step for students to reconcile themselves with their traumatic past and overcome the relational distance that has hardened their hearts and minds over the years. By embracing a more constructive approach to conflict, students rediscover the humanity they share with the neighbors they once considered enemies.

Chapter 4, "Putting the Relational Model to the Test," tackles the need to challenge the ongoing distortions and illusions that govern how students perceive one another. Psychological illusions, "mirages" as he calls them (*miraggio*), fantasies and mental constructs must be healed because they *re-present* for students their polarizations and emotional blackmails. Conversely, trust, desire for change, and dialogue—these three rooted in their shared human suffering—become the building blocks that students must embrace to create relational spaces capable of bridging misunderstandings and facilitating compassionate caring.

Finally, in chapter 5, "Some Final Thoughts and Next Steps," Vaccari concludes the discussion of the Rondine Method, highlighting the nurturing interactions between the parties that are necessary to overcome the obstacles that keep people from personal transformation. Especially valuable to deepening our understanding of the Rondine Method is Vaccari's discussion of five key practical ways to create a permanent "home" environment, within and beyond Rondine. This home environment fosters mutual trust and encourages the practice of hospitality: (1) cracking the firewall that separates people, (2) dissolving the fabricated enemies, (3) overcoming helplessness, (4) transforming pain, and (5) moving beyond victimhood. Because the Rondine Method is open to ongoing theoretical assessments and growth in experiential wisdom, this chapter provides a springboard to consider ways to expand the method with other participants and in other contexts.

The second part of this book, chapters 6 through 9, offers scholarly responses to the Rondine Method. These chapters are not intended to exhaust the possibilities of engaging in critical conversations with the Rondine Method. They provide responses into the kind of reception that this unique approach to conflict has already received among prominent Italian and U.S. voices. These chapters evaluate this method from the perspective of social scientists, psychologists, and scholars who are familiar with this method or have an interest in or have been directly invested in the work of peacebuilding. Thus, these chapters provide a sample of how to place Rondine's contact theory approach in dialogue with valuable insights that scholars and practitioners in the area of conflict resolution have done in various fields. The presence of these voices deepens and expands existing understandings of this unique methodology. The book concludes with Charles Hauss's invitation to the reader to consider Rondine's broad implications and ongoing relevance, especially regarding the method's potential for use in settings in which students experiencing conflict are not able to leave their communities and its potential relevance to address other forms of human polarization and divisions.

Concluding Words: When Strangers Become Angels

I began this introduction alluding to the interpersonal actions of Abraham and Sarah as recounted in Genesis 18. This biblical text tells us that they "hastened" to offer hospitality to the three strangers who visited their home (Gen. 18:6). From the moment they arrive, Rondine invites students to *convivenza*, the daily way of being and living in community that prepares them to hasten and more readily practice hospitality toward all their neighbors, especially those they have considered their enemies. At Rondine so-called enemies recline around a common table. And this physical and relational spontaneous coming together brings students into conversations and personal life-transforming encounters. Rondine invites students to leave behind their cultures of hostility and step into cultures of hospitality. At Rondine, strangers become angel-like figures to one another, messengers of God if you will, who carry, as is the case in the story of Abraham and Sarah, the promise of new life and peaceful coexistence in a world that continues to be scarred by violence, war, and conflict. The Rondine Method offers a "catholic," that is, an inclusive and interpersonal approach, to peacebuilding that addresses the pervasive conflict and polarization that characterizes "the signs of the times."[2] Indeed,

> At a time when the world desperately needs new recipes for success to overcome conflict and promote peaceful co-existence, Rondine's

popular diplomacy offers an interpersonal, interreligious, and intercultural transformative approach for birthing authentic human relationships. Above all, this approach promotes an integral ecology of life among diverse, but all too often, estranged neighbors who inhabit the same common home. Scholars, diplomats, religious voices, civil servants, and world leaders can all learn from Rondine's unique method of discovering the "person" in one's unknown neighbor. (Appleby and Cizik 2015)

Over the years, my appreciation for the Rondine Method has grown not only because of my interest in diplomacy and my desire to advance human rights but also because of my professional background as a Catholic theologian. Few would question the role that religion exercises in global affairs. Religion has often been manipulated to divide us, but religion can also serve as a force for good to bridge human differences. Engaging religious communities is essential to address conflict and bring about lasting peace (bin Muhammad and Yarrington 2010). In this sense, while the Rondine Method is not explicitly religious—it is not faith-based diplomacy—its focus on hospitality and dialogue taps into some of the world's religions' most basic common and sacred words, namely, the love of our neighbors (bin Muhammad and Yarrington 2010). In my view, the Rondine Method translates this commonly held religious principle into a vernacular expression that many people can share. This unique bridge-building recipe is much needed today to address local, regional, and international conflicts. I see the Rondine Method, and what it represents regarding addressing human conflicts, as a gift with the potential to offer us a more just, ecologically friendly, and peace-filled common home, capable of reconstituting the relational life of its inhabitants (Pope Francis 2015).

Notes

1. See also Goizueta's discussion of Aristotle's distinction between "praxis" as an activity that is an end in itself and "poiesis" as an activity that places value in production, the by-product of human action. As Goizueta argues in this discussion, the difference between praxis and poiesis is also analogous to that between playing a musical instrument and *making* a musical instrument.

2. The term "signs of the times" comes from Vatican II, the Roman Catholic gathering of bishops (1962–1965) convened to address, among other things, the challenges faced by Roman Catholics in modern times. See *Gaudium et Spes*, n. 4. For a Catholic approach to peacebuilding very much in the spirit of Vatican II, see Schreiter et al. (2010).

Part 1

THE RONDINE METHOD

CHAPTER 1

The Steps toward Trust[1]

Franco Vaccari

In the spring of 2018, the Permanent Mission of Italy to the UN invited Rondine Cittadella della Pace to tell the story of its peacebuilding efforts to the Secretariat on December 10 at an event that commemorated the seventieth anniversary of the adoption of the Universal Declaration of Human Rights. That day, several of Rondine's former students spoke in the name of those who were unable to do so themselves and who continue to die because of the horrors of war.

Rondine is a medieval hamlet in Tuscany, a place where the commitment to a set of psycho-pedagogical practices has allowed us to create the Rondine Method.[2] For over two decades, young people from all over the world have been coming here to attend a two-year educational-training program offered at our World House.[3] These young people wish to change themselves, and they wish to change the relationships among all people who are caught up in those wars and transform the wounds caused by hatred into friendship and peacebuilding.

The invitation had inspired many of them to create the three-year Leaders for Peace global campaign, which was launched at the UN that day. The campaign was intended to be a tangible pledge to train young leaders for peace so that they could gain the skills that would allow them to intervene in the world's ongoing conflicts. In practice, the young leaders for peace called on all states to devote a symbolic amount of money from their defense budgets and invest it in scholarships for educational programs on conflict prevention, dialogue, and human rights. That is why Rondine's young people had come to speak to representatives of the UN's 193 member states on behalf of those who cannot yet speak of the "right to peace."

Their appeal was based on twenty years of experience that I had already distilled into a book, the Italian–English *The Rondine Method: Creative Transformation of Conflicts*, which gained some interest beyond Italy. Professor Susan Allen from George Mason University in Fairfax, Virginia, who had known Cittadella

della Pace for some time, for example, wrote an afterword in which she identified a radical change of consciousness as one of the most innovative features of the Rondine method in the search for conflict resolution.

> The openness that occurs when the suffering person is seen in the "enemy" is a sign of a radical change of consciousness. The "enemy" is no longer seen merely as such, but just as a suffering person. (Allen 2018, 330)[4]

I now want to use this chapter and the four that follow to present the Rondine Method in a shorter form, which could be of interest to a broader audience in the English-speaking world.

The Right to Speak Words of Peace

The young students who made the trip to the UN that day had first met in a neutral space: in the village of Rondine Cittadella della Pace. They had lived there together while attending a two-year program in which they committed themselves to no longer seeing each other as enemies, preferring instead to become well disposed toward "the ones over there," the (constructed) enemies who live beyond the borders of their minds.

The students are relatives and friends of war victims for whom they have every right to speak because—mostly as young children—they witnessed the death of fellow citizens. Today, as adults, they still see the rubble in the streets despite ongoing peace processes. They are young people who do not accept the stalemate, and they keep working to open or accelerate the path to reconciliation. They are young people who "allow other voices to speak" while trying to defend themselves from the seed of the poisoned and bloody memories they still carry.

Among the many young people we have worked with, I often recall Ilez, one of the first participants, who came from Ingushetia—a small republic in the Russian Federation and the scene of a bloody conflict in 1992. One day, emerging from his deep silence, he stopped me in the village square at Rondine and asked me, and himself: "Am I the only one left of my twenty classmates from home? Why?" Today, in Rondine, we are asking ourselves why the UN chose us from the many organizations that have spent decades defending human rights, among the many people forgotten and persecuted, imprisoned, and tortured. Why us?

Two words come to mind whenever I think about questions like that: representatives and witnesses. When spoken together by free and responsible people at places like Rondine, these words let young people explore tragic experiences without being overwhelmed by them. They become representatives of peoples, ethnic groups, cultures, traditions, and religions who have witnessed violence, persecutions, crimes against humanity, intolerable pain, and injustice. But they are also representatives of the quest for peace and witnesses of a possible reconciliation. Great strength is needed:

- to look at the wounds of hatred and the poison of enmity
- to generate a change in interpersonal relationships
- to become bearers of hope charged with a future we can begin to build today
- to imagine that future's cultural, social, and political repercussions together

Without courage, which frees their present from the "prison" of the past, those young people would have become defeatists or worse, victims of a creeping or full-blown depression. Despite everything, that courage gives them the right to speak about peace. The choice of engaging with pain is decisive. It is the first step toward avoiding being overwhelmed and toward caring for oneself, searching for concrete alternatives beginning with questions that get at the very core of what makes us human. "What can I do?" "What can we do?"

Rondine empowers its students to embark on the "first steps" taken by people who today feel ready to dismantle the logic of war. They offer themselves to the world not because they have understood all there is to know about "how peace is made" (quite the opposite) but because they have met the enemy in the flesh and found out that the propaganda from both sides had deceived them. This is the fundamental mission that not only legitimizes Rondine's vital call at the UN but helps us all see how the research on the Rondine Method discussed in the rest of part 1 helps us to creatively transform conflict.

The first cycle of studies conducted on the Rondine Method by the Catholic University of the Sacred Heart of Milan and the University of Padua was collected in a volume published by Il Mulino, one of Italy's leading publishers. The research, funded by Vodafone Italia Foundation,

> wanted to investigate, with the support of psychology and philosophy, the peculiarities that distinguish this reality . . . on the one hand "measuring" the changes that animate the intergroup conflicts; on the other, "verifying" the generative scope of the categories of restorative justice outside a criminal context. (Alici 2019, 11)

The First Steps of Trust

The young people who come to the World House at Rondine are the "representatives" of the dissolution of the enemy's deception and "witnesses" of how that way of thinking can be reversed by ordinary people. Places affected by armed conflict are not lacking in hope. They just need young people to go home, look into the others' eyes and see them as whole persons, and listen to them without prejudice so that worn-out relationships can change in an instant, paving a new path forward. The moment when they decide to act can be surprising: "Enough! I have to do something to change."

The decision to connect with the enemy without destroying oneself can lead to trust that "the other" will remain a person, even if mutual hostility lingers. This is the first step. Whether they explicitly realize it or not, this is what they see from the moment that they read about Rondine online. We call on them to make a new beginning, or rather a bright opening, from which a better future can gradually unfold. I have written elsewhere:

> They leave to the past those who have worked to mark with blood the history of their people and with sorrow their life's suffering. If not, they would not apply to Rondine, submitting to an interview in their country before a committee which, sometimes and whenever possible, includes a young person from the enemy side. (Vaccari 2018b, 62–63)

The terms of our agreement with the students are laid out in the invitation to come to Rondine and in the discussions we have once they arrive. With the support of an educational environment at Cittadella della Pace, we offer them the opportunity to live for two years in a community, along with a member of the enemy party with whom they will learn that establishing interpersonal relationships from scratch can open concrete possibilities for collaboration after they go back home. The penultimate paragraph of the invitation introduces the "social impact project," which aims to support their return home. We choose students to come to Rondine by "starting from the end result," identifying young people who intend to return home to make an impact within their society and, above all, to spread a culture of dialogue and reconciliation.

Every year between fifteen and twenty students join the group that arrived the previous year. That creates a turnover in which the "old" and the "new" students have a year in common (they call each other "generations"). As a result, the World House student dormitories are normally home to about thirty-five young people (that number will grow to fifty in the next three years). They are also grouped into pairs from places where ongoing or recently ended war makes positive relationships among individuals from the opposing parties all but impossible.

An account written in 2012 by Elmira, one of the students from Azerbaijan, demonstrates how a "first step" introducing a new and previously unknown psychological and cultural perspective can be made. It takes the strength arising from new defenses against an often-devastating pain to break a rigid pattern of identity and belonging imposed by a group and strengthened by a climate of insecurity and fear.

> We are war children. Our childhood was not spent under the sun; our childhood is an infinitely dark period when dolls are bullet splinters. . . . We grew up with pain in our souls, under the propaganda of hatred towards the enemy, and perhaps we do have the right to hate them. But we "Rondini" have chosen another path, the path of forgiveness. I am a Rondine too [By now, I am already a grown-up Rondine ready to fly, nonetheless a Rondine that remembers and will never forget its story, the story of the small revolution that changed the world, its world. But not everything has been so easy. Do you know what it means to live a lifetime with a clear idea? To be sure of something, to have no doubts, be convinced that you are right? To see—as a child—the blood, tears, and funerals of hundreds of people on the same day; understand that all this pain is to be blamed on those who are on the other side of the border.
>
> I remember that day as if it were yesterday. A normal day in May, a day that didn't seem to be special, but showed me something I had never seen before, which made me understand what I had never understood before. Only "one day" that changed my life. It was a special event with many young people. I was happy to be there, smiling I turned left and right, greeted, shook hands . . . and then stop! Everything stopped. That boy, standing in front of me with that hat and that "Yerevan" inscription. I stopped smiling. "I'm Armenian," he said, challenging me. I no longer saw anyone, only him. Hate—the only thing I saw in his eyes. Hate—the only thing I felt in my heart. "I am Azerbaijani," I said, stressing each syllable. An Azerbaijani and an Armenian, together, close, face to face, eye-to-eye for the first time in our lives. There! In our countries, it would have been impossible. But today this too has happened. (Alici 2019, 181–83)

When these young people chose Rondine, they broke away from family, religious, and political loyalties. People who hang on to a rigid mindset do it to feel secure. When breaking away from it, they face uncertainty. Thus begins a time of transition and personal "migration" when a real exodus takes place that makes anyone feel like a stranger both at home and in the place they are going to, between regrets for "when it was better" and longings for the novelty of an unknown Promised Land. It is a time that calls for genuine authenticity.

"Why on earth did I do it?" is the evocative question that they have to keep asking themselves throughout the transition—until the person finds an answer within themselves. Everyone must accept the long struggle to move ahead if they do not want to move backward and lose all their progress. It is the personal goal adopted by those young people who acknowledge themselves as "migrants" who assume a risky new identity after rejecting the poison that they inherited from their elders. Here is how Miloŝ, from Serbia, helps us keep this migration and human relationships together:

> I imagined a brave, romantic, and above all a glorious death almost every day, the death that would be a source of pride for my family. The horrors of war leave us devastated, dead and wounded. Those who survive live again, who knows how many times it has happened. Human persons alive and, therefore, lucky, but deeply affected, changed, silent, restless, now aware that the horror has ended only temporarily. The overpriced experience has taught them that life in this turbulent area of the world needs persons suited for it. Hate and love cannot coexist in the heart of a human being. When hatred grows, there is no place for love; when pride rises, compassion diminishes. A person under constant threat loses lightness and joy of living. Thus, the fate of our ancestors becomes our destiny. And we all suffer incessantly. The real conflict, the one outside us, creates our internal horizons, giving strength to a vicious circle, whereby the prospect of war becomes the only possible solution. I am in Rondine to move out of this spiral of hate. I am here because hope must win over fate. (Alici 2019, 187–88)

Rondine is a place where everyone—young people, staff, volunteers, and partners—can live their new beginning in which, paraphrasing Hannah Arendt, something new comes to life and opens a space of freedom. This concept applies to everyone, not only to young people like our students. In every interpersonal relationship, there is always an "enemy" in whom we can (re)discover the person who is, above all, a person suffering like us.

We often tell a story that shows how the way that Rondine was born bears witness to what it feels like for people to be united in conflict, even when it has degenerated into violence or war. On a late summer evening in 1997, Professor Mukadi Izrailov, then rector of the University of Grozny and one of the architects of a failed mediation initiative during the war in Chechnya, called me to ask: "Can you accept some university students? Our kids can no longer study in Moscow; we are trying to send the best abroad." "Yes," I immediately replied, "if they agree to come with the Russians." "Ah, it's not a problem for us as long as you can find a Russian who will sleep in the same room with a Chechen!" My answer was spontaneous, and some remember it as ingenious, perhaps due to the destabilizing impact welcoming these university students would have on everyone. They had asked for a year of hospitality and ended up with a project beyond their expectations. Because it is here between one's conscience and vision that one discovers the difference between "taking a step" and "taking the first step" (Vaccari 2018c, 21–24).

We met the challenge. Russian friends in St. Petersburg and Moscow quickly found two students who were willing to "sleep in the same room with the Chechens": Sergei and Ilia from St. Petersburg and Krasnodar, which is not far from the Caucasian regions and Chechnya. Sergei had lost relatives, and members of Ilia's family had fought in the Russo-Chechen war. Both arrived in Rondine having agreed to spend a year with the Chechen students Murad, Muslim, and Akhmed who had also lived through the tragedy. Those five little yeses mark the beginning of the International Student Hall (now the World House), which is the physical heart of Rondine Cittadella della Pace. It was a birth "managed" with great innocence on all sides. Nonetheless, trust—the yeast of every relationship—now makes its way into everything we do, as you will see in the rest of part 1.

"Finding the Russians" meant walking into the "peace forest" to open a more accessible path for everyone. Thus, Rondine managed to fulfill the desire of a personal friend of mine, the Russian academic Dmitry Sergeyevich Likhachov, a scholar who had spent eleven years in a Soviet gulag. It all happened in a way that neither of us had imagined when in 1993, at our neighbor, the Franciscan Sanctuary in La Verna, Likhachov issued an appeal: "Call the people here to make peace." In 1997, we started with a few people after progress was interrupted by the failure of behind-the-scenes peace negotiations in 1995. Two years later, five young university students boarded three civilian airplanes rather than the Italian Red Cross aircraft that would have carried the official negotiators from the Russian and Chechen governments if an agreement brokered by the Italian Senate Foreign Affairs Committee and the Italian Ministry of Foreign Affairs had been accepted. In La Verna, the five young people did not enter into secret negotiations. They simply started living together, sleeping under the same roof, studying together, and sharing meals in Rondine in an environment where words of peace take on real meaning.

When you put aside the heroic but often unachievable myth of elite diplomacy, you open the door to the authentic construction of a dream. That series of first steps and the yes uttered by those students can silence all the "buts" because it is those yeses that make history. Their consent reinforces the most authentic vision of popular diplomacy. These are not extraordinary people engineering unheard of events. Rather, every man, every woman, even in a powerless social condition (young people!), can intervene to give a different direction to the events, even the most tragic conflicts.

After this twenty-year-long journey together, we are now convinced that there are no more excuses. Everyone can achieve peace. On October 16, 1998, the Cittadella della Pace was inaugurated in the village of Rondine. Those first steps may not have been fully planned, but they emerged full of life and became the cornerstone of our community.

BUILDING MUTUAL TRUST

We created the World House Student Residence on the assumption that a "true" relationship between two young enemies and strangers could lead to a significant change between the larger groups that they come from. By shifting from hostility to collaboration, one generates enough trust in the other that it can be turned into deep friendships.

The Rondine Method is based on the proven assertion that mutual trust fosters an intense and creative bond that grows out of the interaction between young people in a supportive educational environment. Educational, psycho-pedagogical, and social practices can foster adult dialogue that removes the oppressive dependency in which everything revolves around one's identity. Trust toward one another is like the invisible soul of our relational nature, without the hassle of rigid constraints (Hegel, cited in Natoli 2016, 82). Consequently, creating that environment and the reciprocity of trust are the two basic requirements for putting the Rondine Method into practice. We will approach them separately in the discussion that follows so that you can grasp the unique role of the "relational facilitator," whose work is quite different from that of a mediator, who seeks agreement between the parties.

Rondine: A Trust-Facilitating Environment

The training environment at Rondine includes the educational staff and the young people who come from about twenty-five war-torn countries. However, without trusting one another, the hospitality we offer in itself would not trigger the desire for a stable relationship:

> Trust moves through one's personal life, energizing the most secret depths of our intimacy, and generates relationships that establish a new way of being together, feeding social ties and public institutions. Trusting testifies to the initial opening of reciprocity in which we are rooted and the chance of envisioning, within a creative tension, the anthropological, ethical and political challenges of fragility, difference, and coexistence. (Alici 2018, back cover)

Because of the stability that can be provided at a place like Rondine, the inner strength that comes from familiarity between two people does not disappear. Instead, it expands as it matures in the space–time of daily sharing:

> Trust seems to possess a certain unconditional feature: in fact, its prominent place is friendship. Here trusting is entrusting and even giving oneself. The extent to which trust is involved in friendship and friendship in trust derives from how the Greek term philia (friend-

ship) is used. Originally, rather than referring to a privileged personal relationship—as it will be discussed later—it had an eminently social meaning. It indicated hospitality, that is, the capacity and above all the obligation to welcome, and consequently, the philia relationship established between the host and the hosted. (Natoli 2016, 59–60)

The experience gathered from my three professions (psychologist, teacher, and trainer) resulted in the search for new and different cultural paradigms that provide mental magnifying glasses through which we make sense of the world and its conflicts. While the Rondine Method has most of its roots in psychology and pedagogy, the tools we use and their theoretical underpinnings also draw on philosophical anthropology and theology.

To understand the choices that we made in developing the Rondine Method in which different types of trust building interconnect, we have found it useful to refer to Erik Erikson's (1950) eight-stage theory of psychosocial development.

Erikson focused on two portions of any person's life cycle that proved particularly useful for our purposes. The first stage (zero to two years old) is decisive for trust building; in turn, the transition from any one stage to another is a moment of crisis that allows, under favorable conditions, for the recovery and development of what had previously remained unexpressed. Indeed, it can lead to a more substantial intrapsychic unity through which the individual becomes capable of overcoming earlier negative experiences. The young people at Rondine experience this dynamic among themselves. In the first six months, they go through a sort of regression in a safe place in which learning an entirely new language (Italian) is an essential part of the process. They also experience a critical period of transition that can be identified by appealing to Erikson's sixth and seventh stages. It is a transition from youth, characterized with its polarity between intimacy and isolation into adulthood, which unfolds between generativity and stagnation (twenty-three to twenty-eight years).

In the first stage, the child's growth depends on the polarity of playfulness between trust and mistrust. Primarily constructive experiences can lead to the creation of a stable and positive personality trait that Erikson calls hope. It will gradually replace the prevailing negative mistrust that exists due to the frustration the child suffered that had produced an aggressive and/or defiant attitude. Thus, as the psychological dynamic of the first stage centered on trust reemerges, the young student at Rondine blends the crisis of the transition between the sixth and seventh stages. It becomes clear that strong generativity can be created simply by building confidence. Indeed, given that the shift was considered impossible in the home environments from which they came, the individual can acquire incredible strength by experiencing the crisis through forging a new relationship with a person previously presumed to be an enemy.

In acknowledging each other as different, the young people also experience mutual trust at Rondine. This step is essential for cultivating friendship and developing collaborative projects that they can undertake together based on a tangible foundation and exchange that takes place between concrete and diverse individuals. Comparing Rondine to the other professional fields mentioned above, we have demonstrated significant value on a psychosocial, but perhaps also an anthropological, level. When a person becomes aware of being sensitive and open to diversity as a "concept," that is, as a cultural conviction, we are still not sure that that person can acknowledge the relationship with another person "in person." In this sense, trust, granted to the other, becomes a real attitude only within a stable bond with what we call a "different-concrete" person.

This is an essential transformation for anyone who has lived through the traumatizing experience of war or has grown up in a postwar social environment. For young people, developing this type of relationship is the only possible pathway toward preserving the hope of giving birth to an alternative experience.

Therefore, from the beginning of the two-year program, young people meet a multiplicity of different-concrete people and make a deliberate choice to build relationships rather than preoccupying themselves with what psychologists call the image of the enemy. Forging those relationships not only involves members of the educational staff but also includes their peers at the World House who come from a dozen cultures and nationalities. Coming from these places, they all participate in the deconstruction of hatred toward those they have heretofore referred to as an enemy and with those volunteers of different ages and social status that embody expressions of the local culture.

These ways of relating fit the anthropological paradigm of hospitality that invites each student to become jointly responsible for their own healing. However, belonging to the "world of Rondine" is not the ultimate goal. Instead, we hope the students develop a new and dynamic identity within a new cultural space that gets translated into the strengthening of an open mind while augmenting their links with their original culture. We never intended for Rondine Cittadella della Pace to turn into a cosmopolitan international movement. Rather, we want it to remain a unique place, where we continue to refine our ability to help young people develop autonomous experiences that respect their diversity and thus, their differences.

The Rondine Training Course

Our curriculum builds on the starting point I just discussed. The Rondine Method helps students redefine their relationship with each other and with their own lived experiences on the basis of a common commitment to:

- reducing armed conflicts in the world
- disseminating the Rondine Method with the goal of creatively transforming conflicts everywhere

In short, our goal has been to create an approach that is rooted in local experiences but has the capacity to make Rondine an "interlocutor of the theory and practice of the transformation of conflicts on a global level" (Allen 2018, 329). Above all, "this approach promotes an integral ecology of life among diverse but all too often, estranged neighbors who inhabit the same common home" (Díaz 2018, 47). This first result is achieved through the two-year training course, which is divided into four phases. Starting from the experience of war, it aims to transform conflicts through interpersonal experiences.

The first is a trial period (from July to the end of September). The training focuses on the intensive study of Italian, the creation of group identity, and the introduction of the Rondine Method's core concepts. During this period, the students also figure out whether the realities of life at Rondine meet their hopes and expectations. At the same time, the staff determines whether the participants meet their expectations, especially the desire for coexistence with the enemy, before helping the students choose the master's degree program they will pursue. In other words, beginning to create the new mindset comes before any career choice.

The second phase occurs during the first academic year from October to June. The program includes classes and other activities that focus mainly on conflict, war, and human rights; the acquisition of communication skills; facilitation within the group; and the analysis of oneself and one's emotions. Students must be able to use the tools we provide to experience the differences within the group that reflect the reality of globalization as lived at the scale of a tiny village in Tuscany. At the end of the first year, we assess their progress toward several objectives, including their:

- ability to manage interpersonal conflicts
- willingness to talk about their experience
- emotional intelligence
- awareness of their own conflicts
- performance and participation in internal training
- internalization of the Rondine Method
- leadership potential

The third phase takes place during the summer break between mid-July and September. The time away from Rondine, especially if spent with their families and therefore in their own country, can be difficult because it provides the first opportunity to test how much the individual student has changed and become open to a dialog with those who do not live in the Rondine bubble. The break thus provides practical experience or a laboratory through which the young people from the World House can carry out a self-assessment of what they have learned and, if needed, to confirm their decision to stay at Rondine.

The fourth and final phase comes as part of the second-year training program (September to June) and continues to focus on their personal growth but adds what might be called an outward dimension that anticipates their return home:

- enhancing their awareness of the ways in which their identity has evolved
- identifying their professional "vocation" by focusing on leadership skills, especially by mentoring the new "generation" of students who arrive at about that time
- preparing for their return to their home countries where they will put their social impact projects into practice
- determining if they have met all the criteria for becoming members of the Rondine International Peace Lab, which is the association of "Rondine d'Oro" as students who have successfully completed the two-year course are known.

An Example of Political Transferability: The Rondine d'Oro in Sierra Leone

Nine young people from Sierra Leone (two of whom have since died) were trained at the World House Student Residence during the 2010s. Sierra Leone experienced a civil war between 1991 and 2002 that killed at least 50,000 people. It then went through a difficult reconstruction period during which the Ebola virus struck, adding another 4,000 victims.

In anticipation of the presidential elections held in March–April 2018, the seven remaining former enemies from Sierra Leone and other Rondine d'Oro undertook a two-year project to engage the population and political leaders in a campaign to prevent violence and to convince all parties to accept the results of the election. That task force of former enemies and former students at Rondine (Sierra Leoneans from the south and north but also Lebanese, Kosovars, and Azerbaijanis) adopted the slogan of "One voice, one vote, no violence." The campaign encouraged respect for one's political rival and called on people to act responsibly and not vote automatically for candidates who were members of the voter's tribe.

The former enemies crisscrossed the country's fourteen districts, hosting community meetings, holding round tables at the universities, and using media and social networks. The campaign reached the most remote regions of Sierra Leone, including villages that had never before been visited by any international organization. The team had one-on-one discussions with around 700 of their fellow citizens and reached about 2.5 million people indirectly. Over 350 highly respected local community leaders received individualized training.

It was a vast and complex experiment that is now receiving widespread recognition for contributing to the maintenance of peace and promoting democracy. Speaking and acting publicly together, the former enemies and the people they worked with caught a glimpse of the Sierra Leone of the future, which they all could support.

> Tony saw his father die when he was a child; he was killed while taking him to school on a bicycle. For a long time, he retraced the same road, meeting the killers every morning. Leonard lost a sister in the war. Tony and Leonard were enemies. Their ethnic groups were the Temne, concentrated in the north-west, and the Mende, in the south-east. The project's local partner was precisely the University of Makeni, where Tony, a teacher, and Leonard, a librarian, now work. "Being there together during the training of local leaders," Tony says, "has made us the concrete example of how a man from the south and one from the north can live and work together." (Rastelli 2018, 8–9)

They showed their fellow citizens that it is possible to be a faithful member of one's community (tribe, group, people) while simultaneously identifying with a larger political entity (the nation-state) by supporting an inclusive democracy. Research on this experiment in which the Rondine Method was applied to an entire country is underway and could lead to the creation of training courses that local and national leaders could take in any divided country.

Mutual Trust in the Relationship

Earlier, I alluded to the importance of the young people's daily lives during their stay at Rondine, especially the new relationships they can build around the new vision of the world we offer them. That leads to an expansion of mutual trust in everything we do at Rondine and beyond, including in informal encounters that might often seem inconsequential.

For young persons who agree to come to Rondine, that includes every aspect of their lives because we emphasize:

- self-confidence in being involved in promoting wide-ranging social change
- trust in the other, especially the former enemy with whom they share a common space and can become a friend with whom to collaborate
- work with the relational facilitators on the staff to unify the experience with their many connections inside and outside Rondine
- developing trust in their peers in the program who come from other countries (the Caucasus, Balkans, Middle East, Africa) and support each other in the shared commitment to social change in general

As experienced on a daily basis, trust involves risk taking. The investment the young people make plays itself out in three ways, which, if accepted, change them forever:

- acknowledging the importance of moving to Rondine from their far-away home country—"I know why I am here."
- agreeing to engage in a relationship with an unknown person who represents "the other"—"For two years or more, I will have the pleasure/duty of maintaining this relationship."
- overcoming moments of relational and associative crisis—"I am ready and willing to suffer because it is a necessary step toward reaching our goal."

The interconnection between the different types of relationships makes the two-year laboratory at Rondine Cittadella della Pace unusual and perhaps unique. The staff at Rondine has no choice but to operate from an interdisciplinary perspective. The young people we have hosted in recent years have suffered because of severe traumatic episodes in their countries either directly or through their respective families. They have grown up amid tensions and hatred, which have divided their societies over many years, even after the armed conflicts have stopped. We could say they experienced "microtraumas" caused by the disruptive effects of war: daily precariousness, sudden moves, prejudices, and distressing fears. Therefore, it is not surprising that they all come to Rondine with at least latent hostility toward "the other" in ways that vary, of course, from person to person.

So in what sense is mutual trust central? Accepting what we call the "different-concrete" person within the space becomes possible because we help make it happen at Rondine. Over time, that other person, who also has suffered, simultaneously gets ready to give and receive the gift of friendship and to overcome the insults or even the silence that can disturb any new relationship—a point I will return to in more depth in the next chapter.

At this point, it should be clear that mutual trust lies at the heart of any successful relationship. According to the Rondine Method, we have to expect the other to give something of themselves for friendship to become more than just a fantasy. In that sense, I'm often reminded of an African proverb that says: "Alone we are a thread; together we become fabric." Along those same lines, Bishop Nunzio Galantino observes: "A thread does not cover, does not keep us warm, cloth does: in the full experience of reciprocity, the life of the other person concerns me and allows us to create new situations" (2018, 118).

Like Bishop Galantino, we like to use the term *reciprocity*, which is more widely used in Italian than in English, because it adds certainty to any relationship. We like to use that abstract term because of its roots in the Latin *reciprocus*, which implies movement that is both backward and forward. In that sense, "I'm involved, trust me" should not be confused with a command or with statements typical of a utilitarian mindset such as "What do I stand to gain?"

How we make that shift toward trust and all that entails will be the subject of the next chapter.

Notes

1. The five chapters in part 1 are based on earlier works of mine, *The Rondine Method: Creative Transformation of Conflicts* (2018), which was published in an Italian–English edition. The current work is a little over half the length of the original. A version of the *Right to Words of Peace* was published in Luca Alici, ed., *Dentro il conflitto, oltre il nemico. Il "Metodo Rondine"* (Bologna: Editrice il Mulino, 2019). Alici has since become the head of the Rondine Cittadella della Pace Cultural Office.

2. Rondine is the Italian word for *swallow*. We have chosen not to translate the word into English throughout this book to remain faithful to its various usages.

3. The Studentato Internazionale, World House, is at the heart of Rondine: it developed the Citadel of Peace and originated the Rondine Method. Since 1998, it has hosted young people who come from countries where, whether currently or recently, conflict has degenerated into violent forms; they accept to live with their own enemy, therefore facing precisely what they wanted to escape from. Together, they take on a revolutionary path, starting from the pain and the rage resulting from war—to be rediscovered as renewable energy—and elaborating on a creative transformation model. This is developed in three layers: everyday life, educational, and academic. At the end of the two-year period, the youth of the World House have the tools to promote action and develop projects in their own countries and to be leaders in contexts characterized by transformation, elevated complexity, and high conflict. The World House intends to host young people from the five continents as spokespersons of degenerated local conflicts. Currently, it hosts thirty students from twenty-five countries in Europe, Africa, America, and the Near East.

4. I knew about Susan Allen because of her expertise on the armed conflicts of the Caucasus, where about half of the young people hosted in Rondine come from.

CHAPTER 2

The Other Person in the Relationship

Franco Vaccari

The Rondine Method offers the students we accept two years at the World House and with it, an opportunity to learn about an integrated set of psycho-pedagogical practices that we have developed through more than twenty years of multidisciplinary research. As we make clear to our students, it is not simply a list of practices. The method represents a holistic approach that contributes to all aspects of human development.[1] Or as Daniel Rothbart has observed, Rondine can be seen as a "collector of all humanity."

The individual's positivity and uniqueness make the presence of what we call the "different-concrete" other person all the more important when a major crisis occurs. As a result, the training experience is subject to constant review and adaptation because we involve the young people as cocreators and not merely as recipients or beneficiaries of the curriculum.

This statement, written by Sarah, a woman from Lebanon, makes this point more clearly than I can:

> Diversity was our treasure: each person was unique; we all were different. We understood that we had to find common ground to work on, instead of allowing the differences to isolate us in our identities and closed interests. For this reason, the student selection carried out by the Rondine staff is essential; the students must be unique, varied, and they should not aim only at developing their sectorial skills linked to peace-building. To attend Rondine, the applicant must be sincerely ready to simply "be": to be involved; you, your whole being, and not only with your ambitions, your performances, or your education. You must want to take on a new challenge; that is how Rondine works. I was Sarah, and I was not the "Sarah, who wants to do a master's degree in Italy." The master's degree is an important reason, and Rondine is an opportunity for one's CV. However, it is also

important to realize that you must show up as a person and you must be physically here, and you must be bare. We were unveiled, with our feelings. We were transparent. (Vaccari and Simeoni 2019, 162)

The Training Process at Rondine: An Overview

Five key concepts underlie the Rondine Method and its hope for human renewal. The terms make pedagogical sense whether one uses linear thinking, where one concept logically follows the other, or circular thinking, in which each idea both follows and precedes the others. In either event, these five words should be seen as pathways to understanding the Rondine's educational-training experience and what we call its reparative paradigm.

Relationship is the basic desire to meet like-minded people and, therefore, to sustain a human connection. If an interpersonal relationship remains open to any eventuality, however disruptive, it becomes stable and can lead to friendship, which is the feeling of mutual trust par excellence. In the public arena, it makes coexistence possible, creating a more inclusive democracy. In addition, if people respect others' freedom in the heat of a conflict-laden moment, they can reach the fullness of life itself.

Person refers to the *becoming* of the whole human being. From an educational perspective, one is "a potential" person at birth. Thanks to interactions with family and friends, the awareness of one's own and the other person's uniqueness develops over time ever afterward. It is primarily in times of change or crisis, however, that we can learn how to take responsibility for being a free human being. It is then that we can build stronger relationships between two people as well as among a few or many people, thus helping us learn how to be our true self and thereby embrace authenticity both personally and within the social sphere.

Community is the place of proximity and belonging. Experiencing "through" and "beyond" the encounter with other persons and other "neighbors" by opening up toward those who are "distant" can lead us to adopt what could be called an evolutionary identity. Because people feel protected, they can rise to the challenge of opening up to the social world and transcend the troubles they face at the moment.

Politics involves social action that takes individuals beyond their immediate circle by considering the common good or, more accurately, planet Earth's "common goods," from "mine" to "ours" and then to "theirs." Acting politically involves becoming citizens of the world, "cosmopolitans" who think and act in ways that take them beyond the goals and interests of any local area's boundaries. It means moving toward the entire human family and beyond the present time. It means moving toward future generations. Countries at war and societies struggling to survive under what amounts to only a fragile peace have one thing in common—the legacy of poisoned memories. If they want to get past those memories, they have to adopt a different approach to making sense of the facts. Under these circumstances, constructive political action requires individuals both to take responsibility for their own actions and to get past any sense that they are simply victims.

Celebrations can be quasi-magical experiences that include everyone in rites that respect diversity and blend beauty with strength. That "blend" allows us to celebrate all of life, even its pain. A feast, for example, can be seen as an *alternative space–time* that creatively regenerates daily life. When it is a solemn event in which everyone wholeheartedly participates, the feast helps surface the depth of a person's soul that goes above and beyond any religious rituals.

You can get a quick glimpse of the method with a different example. In 2015, Rondine started another experimental course: the Fourth High School Year of Excellence for students in their next to last year of secondary school, which normally takes five years in Italy. In the 1960s, the Italian Ministry of Education formally approved study abroad exchange programs. The fourth-year high school program accepts twenty-five to thirty students from every Italian region for a study abroad program that takes place at Rondine rather than in a foreign country. A specially designed curriculum, "the Ulysses Path," includes an ongoing relationship with the students at the World House and an interdisciplinary curriculum integrated into their high school program at Rondine.

Alternative didactic modules, centered on peace, solidarity, rights, legality, the digital world, and career services, enable teenagers to develop in-depth knowledge of *themselves in close contact with each other*. The anthropological–pedagogical program aims at steadily dismantling prejudices, precursors of the "enemy's" deception, and learning to manage conflicts around certain sets representing "difference": male–female, strong–weak, rich–poor, north–south, foreign–native, simple–complex, fast–slow, analog–digital. The ultimate aim is to overcome the mentality of contrast and enable cooperative projects in severe conflict environments.

RELATIONAL SHOCKS

Rondine is an intercultural community where, not surprisingly, people communicate with each other in many ways. That gives the village an amazing wealth of energy, but it can also be tiring. Even more importantly, because we bring together people with different and, at times, opposing points of view, the World House, staff assumes that it will have to deal with regular misunderstandings, discomfort, and conflict. However, the challenge is to help the students (and staff members) manage and overcome those setbacks so that we can best reach Rondine's broader goals.

We refer to such an event as a *relational shock*. It can be a sudden breakdown that only affects a single individual, or it can disrupt a relationship involving two or more members of the community. It typically happens when some external event produces an intense personal reaction on the part of one or more of the students and interrupts the relationships that they had built up during their time at Rondine. Luckily, the crisis is usually short, lasting only a few days, but rarely affects them for more than a few weeks.

Over the years, these relational shocks or triggering events have almost always come from the outside when an event connected with the history or geo-political situation "back home" surfaced old and painful memories. To see what I mean, consider the case of Ulviyya, a young woman from Azerbaijan. When the frozen conflict with Armenia rekindled the war over the disputed territory of Nagorno-Karabakh in 2016, her brother and the brother of a young Armenian woman who was also at Rondine that year told the community that they were leaving for the respective battlegrounds.

One woman from Azerbaijan talked about the event at a *Dissonanze in accordo* (Differences in Harmony) performance, which is "a non-show, show," or an artistic way of presenting Rondine Cittadella della Pace's message. In them, the young people use the visual arts and music to tell part of their story. The following year, she read the extract for us a second time, at which point we recorded it:

> I got off the bus and stopped for a moment on the road leading to Rondine. I heard a loud cry inside me, telling me not to go, not to stay there! I couldn't believe it. The peace which had grown in my heart in Rondine now made no sense; it was just a LIE.
>
> I asked myself: "How could Rondine change our reality if the war that broke out this morning has already produced victims, and the number of casualties is increasing by the hour?" I was afraid to find my brother's and my friends' names among them. I wanted to erase the image of a coffin with the flag on it. I suddenly remembered the words that my mother always repeated to me when I was a child: "If these Armenians were not here, our life would be better." I kept walking, and I kept repeating: "If these Armenians weren't here . . ."
>
> Two Armenian students were waiting for me at Rondine. They could have been my "enemies." That is what they would have been at home at that moment. At the top of the road leading to Rondine, I immediately met one of them, a young man my age. We didn't greet each other: we stared into each other's eyes. It was a deep gaze.
>
> I saw my fear reflected in his eyes, the same anger, and the hatred I felt in my heart. I kept staring into his eyes and saw his pain.
>
> His brother was also fighting on the border.
>
> That is when I understood what peace is for me. It is me worrying about my "enemy's" brother, his mother, and loved ones who cry at

the other end of the conflict, just like my loved ones. An embrace without blaming anyone.

That is what peace is for me today. It is not the absence of conflict, but it is to discover oneself within the other, respect the other, and find a balance.

This account and many others like it support the hypothesis that the public square and the events that take place in it trigger the crises. That only makes sense. When one is suddenly taken out of a private and safe space and ends up at the center of events of historical significance, everything changes. Some of these young people cannot openly display their opinions or emotions. Due to the tensions in their countries, making friends with the enemy can be risky for themselves and their families. When the word *betrayal* emerges from the emotional cultural depths, it is easy for the changes they have made to recede into the background. And the outside events can have this kind of impact in any number of ways, including in the privacy of their own rooms while watching the news on television, surfing the internet, reading a letter, or receiving a telephone call from home.

All young people experience such shocks. Each individual therefore faces an evolutionary challenge to understand and to take responsibility for the consequences of their actions.

Rondine's staff is always on the alert, trying to determine when and how such a mindset moves from the privacy of an individual's thoughts into the public arena. That helps explain why we put so much emphasis on the causes of those triggering shocks that the students experience. We have two reasons for doing this. First, at least at a superficial level, every relationship has a political dimension. Second, Rondine's transformational curriculum invites students to move those private thoughts into the open so that they can develop more appropriate responses to the relational shocks that are bound to arise in a program like ours.

That's why we keep pushing the boundaries of our research. Ulviyya's testimony reveals the depth of these psychological reactions. Because the World House brings together such a diverse community, we have been able to analyze relationship shocks more and more systematically over the years.

A CHANGED APPROACH

In understanding the kind of anger and fear unleashed at the intersection of anthropological and psychological forces, we discovered that the theory of "the improvised public space" can be insufficient and even misleading. The search for a common denominator that unites various experiences and diverse subjects and cultures engaged in armed conflicts across geographic borders will necessarily fall short due to the many ways pain and mourning manifest themselves. We might characterize this effort as a form of hallucination.

Even after months of living side by side, we note that the relationship between the former enemies remains saturated with lots of "as if" statements. As they experience relational shocks in particular, we have noticed that the young adult falls into a common psychological "trap." The individual speaks to and looks at the other but does not fully listen to or see that individual as a whole person "in the flesh." That's why we think of these reactions as delusions or hallucinations even if they do not go so far as to call their basic psychological existence into question. At that moment, the young person literally cannot see the other except as a reflection of the war that has divided their two peoples. Somehow, the other person comes to symbolize the past with all of its anguish, aggression, and, at times, violence. Unless something is done to change things, the relationship between the two people becomes short-circuited.

To "close" the short circuit triggered by an outside event, the individual has to dredge up all of the deeply felt emotions evoked by the image of the enemy and the horrors of war. For this reason, we have to explore things at an intrapsychological level, which cannot be done using logical, rational, or linear tools alone.

You can get a glimpse of how that works in the following statement by Sultan, who goes beyond the hallucinational or delusional attitude he had when he viewed another person as an enemy. Like him, other young people no longer think of themselves as persons—Yahel, Ibrahim, Valentina, Maria, Orkhan, El-mira, etc.—but as an entire people, the Israeli, the Palestinian, the Bosnian, the Serb, the Armenian, and the Azerbaijani.

> I saw Rijuta [the young Indian woman] as soon as I got off the train at Arezzo. After the greetings, we had coffee together while having a very formal conversation. All the while, I was asking myself what could she be thinking. Does she want to kill me? Does she hate me? Is she afraid of me? Why can't I hate her? But I was surprised because she was kind. She gave me lots of advice on living in Italy and living in Rondine. But then I became "THE PATRIOT" again, and I thought: "What a fake!" It was when all the advice from my elders rushed back through my mind, particularly: "they want to kill us." It sent a shiver down my spine, and my heart skipped a beat. I was unprepared for this. I had met my enemies for the first time, I was with them, and I was all by myself, so vulnerable. I was thinking, "I'm so stupid. I should have listened to my parents; I should have stayed home, where the enemy existed only in books and stories!"

Sultan had grown up in a sea of hatred. "As a child, the elders taught me to hate THE ENEMY I had never seen except on television or in history books," which is what he was describing in the statement I just quoted. Sultan had created his own psychosocial and political identity on the delusional assumption that Indians threatened to annihilate the Pakistani people, despite all the evidence to the contrary. We find some version of that common denominator in the ways all of us construct every "enemy" whether we are at war or not. In so doing, we deny that person their full reality as a person, family member, or citizen.

Here, Sultan begins to reject the sudden outburst of memories from his past that led him to fantasize about "enemies" through his first connection with just a single person, Rijuta, who was sitting across the table from him in the café. Later, when he reflected on how he changed, he will realize that his gaze had shifted from the fears lodged in his imagination to the real human being he was getting to know. It would take him a year to understand this as you can see in a statement he made at that time. "Today, while talking to her, I no longer saw the Indian flag but her face."

Sultan's story confirms yet another principle underlying the Rondine Method. The crisis between a new and initially privately held identity and the old one epitomized by the "flag in Rijuta's eyes" is linked to the fact that "waving a flag" invariably leads us to overlook the value of another person, turning oneself and the other into faceless objects. What had happened to Sultan on an intrapsychic level? His first impression even before he arrived in Rondine had terrified him because of the ambivalence he experienced between the possible real-world relationship with a person and the delusional images with which he had been raised. From the beginning of his fantasized dialogue, Sultan's relationship with Rijuta, the Indian "enemy," and with Noam, an Israeli (for him "another enemy") is blocked. "Today, I am dead"—or so he thought.

A ghostly presence looms over such relationships that reflects the way the realities of what we call the "public space" are distorted by familial private spaces, values, and prejudices. To Giorgi, from Georgia, his family members had repeatedly told him from an early age: "They are coming . . . they are coming" when referring to the Russians. In August 2008, the Russian tanks did arrive from North Ossetia, which is part of the Russian Federation, into South Ossetia, which is part of Georgia, stopping thirty-eight kilometers (about twenty miles) as the crow flies from Georgia's capital city, Tbilisi. The mindset Giorgi had grown up with since childhood also came to the surface in Rondine when seemingly insignificant stimuli reignited his anguish. "They're coming!" had become a nightmare. This happened again one day when he was in the vineyard on the edge of Rondine, where the water of the Arno river reminded him of his lake and he saw enemies everywhere. As he put it, "At that moment, even Noam, an Israeli, seemed like an approaching enemy."

When an individual feels as if they are under immediate threat—even in a supportive environment like Rondine—it is safe to say that they are suffering from a hallucination or a ghostly presence that feels like persecution. That "threat" might appear when the person is alone in their room at night, However, it often comes out into the open when dealing with someone from the other side the next day.

Therein lies a paradox. The ghost tends to surface in the presence of another person! Why? The other real individual, the different-concrete one, triggers the process and is immediately canceled and replaced with the other's fantasy. Pain surfaces. No, it gushes out. It is the other recurring element in the relational shocks that young people suffer, even if it is not always directly connected to war and its traumas.

In other words, two unrelated people who belong to two communities in conflict with each other often have attitudes, behaviors, and feelings of hatred that are consistent with what psychologists call the image of the enemy. From their first encounter onward, like Sultan and Rijuta at the railway station, they find themselves face-to-face with a real person. In fact, our training path intentionally starts by having the "pair of enemies" meet each other upon arrival at the Arezzo train station. The "relational migration" begins a journey during which the young people will build trust because they know they are being welcomed into a neutral space by a third party (Rondine) with its staff of trainers, educators, and volunteers.

No matter what they may have heard on the news or even from former Rondine students, no one can truly anticipate what any first encounter with someone from an enemy group will be like. That person, of course, usually was not personally involved in the conflict whether it took the form of a shooting war or a tense armed standoff. Still, the realities the two face is complex. And rarely, as in Sultan's case, does the transformation begin immediately.

From the very beginning of the training course, the two individuals start new relationships along the lines discussed in the previous chapter. We help them bond with each other by starting with the very question of whether they can form such a connection if their image of the enemy persists. In particular, we help them grapple with the reasons why two "innocent" people like themselves simultaneously become both the subject and the object of such hostile attitudes.

Little by little, the residue of hatred they had learned from their "in groups" gives way to the confidence that typically flows from a constructive relationship that emerges both from living together and from Rondine's curriculum, which allows the young people to become normal, healthy people. Critical here is what we call "Rondine after 6:00 p.m.," when the students are free to organize their own activities after they return from their university classes and finish their household chores. This is a time, too, when the village offices are closed and the staff members have gone home. We may call these "informal relations," but they are an important part of Rondine's training program. As we see it, the students' humanity comes to life as it gets freed from the "poisoned" way in which their attitudes toward the other had previously been shaped. The formal training course builds on these first steps by embedding these informal relations into the entire Rondine experience and, thereby, their attitudes toward the other.

Rondine helps the human spirit flourish, and just like grass, it always grows back no matter what you do to try to kill it, even if you pave over it. In other words, it takes extraordinarily little for the best in us to reappear. Still, we know that we cannot forget making that happen is a challenge that can begin with a simple act that cascades and builds on itself.

MOVING TOWARD A RELATIONAL APPROACH TO CONFLICT

The Rondine Method is based on gathering the perspectives of the World House residents, taking their points of view seriously, and focusing on the intrapsychic implications of the trauma they have experienced. As noted earlier, the real events that led to that trauma is what creates the hallucination or ghostly presence that "replaces" the reality of the other person in our students' minds. There are lots of reasons why that is the case, which we have identified in two bodies of scholarly research.

The first centers on the protagonists. In revisiting their traumatic history, the students often feel that they have lost control of their own destiny. They feel overwhelmed and start looking for an escape from the relationship they are building with the other or even from Rondine itself, both of which suddenly have come to feel claustrophobic.

At this point, they face a contradiction between the stereotypes they brought with them to Rondine and the reality of the person standing in front of them. Here, we have to help them find the resources that they are missing when someone "looks without seeing" and "interacts with a ghost," including rationalization, negation, projection, and so on. They must look through the process of constructing and deconstructing their image of the enemy in ways that I will lay out in chapter 4 so that they can best be prepared for their future service to their country as agents for constructive social change after they leave Rondine's supportive environment.

The second research area revolves around the way people interpret the past when they are physically away from home or wherever those events occurred. In our case, war and conflict become a kind of short circuit that blocks healthy relationships and sets off a chain reaction of miscommunication and more, which end up leading to what I have been calling dealing with a ghostly apparition. With our staff's ongoing support, students undergo a form of personal exploration that starts with the need to share—rather than avoid—their pain. Their face-to-face encounters with the other in the form of their fellow students becomes the ideal setting to redefine their deep-seated and intensely held beliefs so that they can have real dialogues, as you will see below.

Something might come up that undermines the relationship between one person and another. Something might be there in the subconscious that the individual may not even be aware of. People are affected by their history and the fear, pain, and anger that they carry, which can turn into a toxic stew that sucks young persons into stereotypes, hatreds, and taboos. However, it is at this point that the two-year residency at Rondine can make a difference because we help the students abandon the stubborn "us versus them" logic and resume their journey toward a new identity and way of life.

On the basis of what we learned from this research, we developed a theory about how relational shocks can lead to a new, transformed outlook on life. Abandoning stereotypes about the enemy and becoming aware of one's negative attitude and behavior are not enough. They also have to overcome the resistance they will face when they return home and have to deal with prejudices again.

The two research strands are inextricably intertwined. They have an obvious common point of departure—the strength of relating to the other that holds up in spite of every challenge and can be triggered by the kinds of traumatizing episodes each of our students has lived through. It is this relationship that is sought after as the place to reconcile these unresolved tensions. At that point, two questions arise. What is happening on a psychological level that produced and reinforces that trauma? How can the individual's mindset change so that the student can put the past into a more constructive perspective?

We use one basic theory in responding to both of those questions. We can build on the "unknowns" in the students' attitudes toward the other to shift their relationship and its dynamics. As you will see in the next chapter, conflict resolution theory enables us to unleash the growth potential in any relationship while helping the students see how deceit and negativity create the short circuit I just discussed. In particular, I will focus on the effort it takes to overcome the pain that occurs when our students go through one of those relational shocks.

Finally, we are well aware that we can never eliminate pain or suffering in today's world. Still, our work over the last twenty years has convinced us that if we want to promote international peace and conflict resolution as an antidote to our traumatic history, we have to set out on a new and different path.

By using the Rondine Method, we hope to overcome the tragic unraveling of human relationships that so often accompanies conflict. We use the Rondine experience to put students on a path toward mutual trust that begins with the small "first steps" discussed so far in part 1.

Note

1. See his discussion in chapter 9.

CHAPTER 3

The Heart of the Rondine Method

THE RELATIONAL APPROACH TO CONFLICT

Franco Vaccari

In the last two chapters, I focused on the ways that a student's experiences lead us to the relational aspects of conflict. As you read about that focus in this chapter, keep some key concepts in mind, most notably, the individual, trust, dialogue, attention, imagination, and cultural creativity. In the process, I hope you will see how and why we blend the philosophical–anthropological with the psychological–pedagogical strands of the behavioral sciences.

The Philosophical–Anthropological Strand

Human renewal is at the heart of the Rondine Method because everyone, everywhere can nurture a welcoming and caring approach to life. In the process of developing our model, we have also learned that any creative and lasting conflict transformation takes place most readily in an environment in which constant care and attention are given to everyone who takes part in a peacebuilding process.

How does such a renewal begin? Our young "former enemies" may come to us at Rondine thinking that they are ready to resist and even overcome the devastating impact of violent conflict. Nevertheless, freedom from victimhood is not enough to bear the brunt of relational shocks that come from face-to-face encounters with the former enemy. As mentioned at the end of the previous chapter, *trust in the dialogue with the other* person is rediscovered in a third or neutral space where young people have chosen to live in "close quarters" with each other for two years. As they deal with our relational approach to conflict, they both rediscover and come to rely on their own unique personalities and identities and, together with that of their erstwhile enemy, "give time" for their relationship to stabilize and mature.

37

To get to that point, our research and extended discussions have helped us to synthesize the work of a number of prominent philosophers and anthropologists, which we have integrated into the Rondine Method.

Choosing to commit to others and accepting their diversity are the cornerstones of the many personalist philosophies developed by the likes of Emmanuel Mounier and Paul Ricoeur. For Mounier (1986), people manifest themselves in making a heartfelt commitment to society, while for Ricoeur (1990), decentralization of the individual is a decisive act every time one accepts to enter into dialogue with others, hoping to feel like persons who walk together in time.

The desire to understand and turn toward the world and toward others defines the individual. This person, materialized in a body and placed in specific historical contexts, accepts responsibility for the present without taking refuge in the past or fleeing into the future. Fostering one's true inner spirit opens social and political horizons beyond anything resembling conservative nostalgia or pseudo-revolutionary dreams.

During such an interaction, the person discovers their own and the other individual's uniqueness. In that moment, the "I" surrenders to a "You," an act that fundamentally forges the relationship because it is anchored in the willingness to converse, and where the human word becomes a nondominating protagonist. In *Zwiesprache* (*I and Thou*), Martin Buber (1937) argues that the word dwells in the silent void lying between interlocutors. It is in-between, in this liminal space, where the "I" gives the "You" the initiative to communicate on the assumption that the "You" is novelty itself, through and beyond all its words. Such a dialogue cannot be confused with a discussion, even a quiet one. It is hard for people who hold divergent points of view to collaborate or even have a rational dialogue. Dialogue requires listening in a way that takes both parties beyond the tangle of rights and wrongs toward a point upon which a true relationship can be based.

Similarly, according to Emmanuel Levinas (1983), the "face" is at the center of any relationship. Being face-to-face allows an individual to view and accept another beyond their social, religious, or any other affiliation. The individual's ongoing curiosity and discovery allows them to shed the illusion that a person's "character" is based on any such simple measurement or category. To the contrary, my fellow human must stand directly in front of me so that I can see our dramatic differences as well as the characteristics that we share. As he saw it, a stable relationship, by definition, includes what can be thought of as distance in mutual closeness in which people preserve themselves by giving themselves to the other.

The "appearance" of the other individual's face comes at the same time that the two parties psychologically surrender to each other. It occurs at a time when both of them leave behind the loneliness they have lived with for so long.

Levinas's thesis about the need and possibility to give each person the time to give birth to a feeling of the other as a neighbor brings to mind the importance of truly listening and, better yet, paying close attention to one's interlocutor. Simone Weil (1950) expresses this idea with her idea of relationality through which one unconditionally listens to and concentrates on what another person says. This is only possible by being "distant in closeness," which can only take place when one turns physically toward wounded people who have been damaged by a war or in some other way. As she saw it, the act of asking questions like "what happened to you" allows one to know that other person as a whole and not simply as a member of a group of people that carry a label such as "unfortunate."

Ivan Illich (2009) sees himself in this paradigm when he suggested the idea of *philia* in which free spirits encounter each other "beyond the set automatisms of recognition and self-recognition." Illich himself suggested that when you listen respectfully and unconditionally, you bow yourself to that person's otherness, and give up looking for emotional barriers separating the two of you. Paradoxically, when we take away those artificial bonds, two people can start a real relationship.

The Psycho-Pedagogical Strand

The Rondine Method is partially based on "the constructive module of psychological consideration [which] brings different perspectives into dialogue," which, in our case, are combined with a number of psychological and pedagogical perspectives (Trevi 1987, 93). From this angle, the human being is seen as part of a *self-re-creation* process in which guided development and what we call self-training extend throughout the traumatized person's lifetime.

Our approach to psychosynthesis is "humanistic" and is thus holistic rather than fragmentary and is meant to bring out each person's potential. It is inspired by a Jungian principle in which one's personality is built around a *unifying center*. Psychosynthesis is a method of psychological development and self-realization for those who refuse to remain the slave of their inner phantasms or of external influences, who refuse to submit passively to the play of psychological forces that is going on within them, and who are determined to become the master of their inner kingdom (Assagioli 2018).

Roberto Assagioli (1888–1974), the founder of psychosynthesis, loved to integrate it with contributions from other psychological schools of thought to the point that, today, it represents a kind of intellectual eclecticism that can be used by just about any practitioner. From the relational approach to conflict theory, we have identified a few authors whose work can be integrated with the essentials of psychosynthesis, including Erik Erikson (1950) and Donald Winnicott (1971) for trust and relationship with one's environment as well as Jung (1916/2003, 1967) and Winnicott again for the relationship between creativity and imagination in the real world.

In more recent years, some psychoanalysts have chosen to examine "inter-personal relationships" in conflict settings more closely:

- Because therapeutic practice involves *listening to pain*, it is hard to understand the causes of a person's trauma without losing one's sense of distance and identifying with the patient.
- Any reflection on their condition invariably takes them beyond the individual's personality.

The theoretical contributions of these schools of thought have to be included in any understanding of a relationship in which two people from opposite sides of a dispute agree to enter into a dialogue with each other.

This statement by an Italian proponent of *bi-personal psychoanalysis* who rethought the therapeutic setting in the light of a paradigm of relationality and was taken even further by another Italian colleague.

> The analytic field is not the *sum* of two internal situations, but something new created *between* two people in the unity that they form together in the session. (Lingiardi 2019, 62)

The Rondine Method extends these ideas beyond a formal psychotherapeutic setting, most notably when a young adult takes part in an emotionally difficult dialogue (cf. Corbella 2005, 16). Other *relational psychoanalysis* research was inspired by two psychiatrists who broke away from the Freudian matrix in the 1920s—Harry Stack Sullivan, who pioneered the relational approach to the interview, and Ludwig Binswanger, who researched how a patient experienced time as part of a clinical practice. In more recent years, this work was brought forward by Stephen Mitchell, who created New York University's Relational Track in its graduate program in psychotherapy and psychoanalysis.

TRUST AND A FACILITATING ENVIRONMENT

This takes me back to chapter 1 where I introduced Erik Erikson's notion of "basic trust." He argued that human beings can only fully reach their potential if they can build a positive image of themselves in the world at that stage in their development. That, in turn, allows them to develop a sense of independence and interdependence through which they can take initiatives in all aspects of their lives.

The "trust-facilitating environment" is one of Donald W. Winnicott's unique contributions. Every psychological progress—from young children to adolescents (and adults, including patients in therapy)—depends on a potential space of experience, which facilitates trust in free interactive play, regulated by simple physical presence.

Winnicott (1971) took these ideas further when he wrote about trust in a "fulfilling environment." Whether you are talking about young children, adolescents, or adults, every psychological development in therapy (or elsewhere) has to be based on expanding what he called a growing space in which individuals add to their reservoir of trust in an environment that encourages safe play and other forms of interaction. As he saw it, no one ever fully comes to grips with reality because there is always some tension between the "external" reality and how the individual perceives it. Parental care can provide that for children. Adults often turn to art or religion to create a meaningful connection between the self and the "real world."

The sociologist Alain Caillé agrees that one needs an environment of trust to truly foster a culture of "giving" in human relationships. Indeed, trust and giving are inseparable in a number of ways, ranging from the instrumental to the contractual as well as the emotional. In his words, "human beings are endowed with the capacity for initiative, independence, and gift" (Caillé 1998, 104). Human relationships are filled with ties that are not simply economic or contractual but in which we trust one another without any expectation of any kind of immediate return, which amounts to the "gift" of mutual trust (Godbout 1998, 22).

FANTASY, IMAGINATION, CREATIVITY, AND CULTURAL EXPERIENCE

Even though they never worked together, both Jung and Winnicott stressed the key role that imagination and a creative mindset play in helping people dream about the future and then share those visions with other people. Here, two key points overlap.

First, imagination and fantasy are not the same. Imagination is a psychological phenomenon through which an individual arranges "images" into potential new realities. By contrast, fantasy produces images that are disconnected from the reality at hand. As Winnicott saw it, children who begin to play invest reality with their own meaning. For Jung, fantasy was simply unreal, a ghost, or a fleeting impression, while imagination carries with it both creativity and a goal one hopes to reach. The two, however, do overlap because imagination can help bring fantasies to life under the right circumstances.

Jung believed that individuals have to develop the possibilities that seemingly random images and dreams can take them to. Imagining and dreaming have a logic that we can see if we are careful not to interrupt the flow of our unconscious. He focused on the "dynamic connections" between the self and the unconscious so that a deeply disturbed patient can (re)integrate those images and dreams and return them to an effective life (Trevi 2012, 24).

Winnicott stressed that dreaming and fantasizing routinely help children under the age of eighteen deal with space and time. What happens in their minds takes place immediately, whether it happens that way in reality or not.

In individuals' psychological life, creativity occupies an intermediate space and forms a matrix that gives their dreams and fantasies a kind of cultural relevance. When and if a maturation process begins, the individuals imagine a new outline of a "shape," which can only fully take form and become visible when they share it with others. Therefore, we speak of transformation as an end product because development or maturation can only occur through a kind of dialogue between the self and the real world.

Creativity can, therefore, be understood as the way symbols are converted from libidinal drives into some higher and more useful form. That said, not every transformation involves a radical change that leads to a definitive outcome. Instead, creativity should be seen as an ongoing and lively process that helps us fill in the blanks when we interpret reality.

The idea of cultural creativity brings Winnicott's and Jung's work together, albeit with some nuanced differences. For Winnicott, fantasy and dreaming remained raw impulses that did little more than incubate new understandings of reality. By contrast, "imagin/action" can keep creativity alive because it brings two people together and begins a new kind of cultural connection. At the end of the day, dreaming and fantasizing are simple individual needs, while imagining is a desire to "move with" and share one's inspiration.

Jung believed that individuation consisted at least of a creative dialogue between the self and a symbolic version of the collective "so that a society's historic values are neither suffered in silence nor ignored, but lived critically and responsibly" (Trevi 2012, 62). Thus, the individual is not simply a single being but is also a by-product of actual social interactions. In that sense, individuation need not lead to isolation but rather a more intense and society-wide solidarity.

The Relational Model

While writing this section of the book, I often found myself returning to Jung's well-known intolerance of our tendency to schematize everything we humans do.[1] Indeed, any attempt to develop a theoretical model suggests that we have to follow a linear sequence that seems to convey a certain logical certainty. However, such a view is at odds with the more fluid and circular reasoning that one finds in persuasive arguments anchored in our lived experience. Therefore, we have sought to create a relational approach to conflict that starts with a few basic steps and gradually adds more complicated issues. In our case, that first meant deciding whether we should start with the interpersonal relationships or the conflict itself, which was not an easy choice to make.

When we dealt with that dilemma, we decided to focus on the trauma that prevents two young, former enemies from coming together. From what they told us in their applications and other statements, I realized that those relations reach their nadir when the conflict and the associated hostility are at their peaks. At Rondine, the students can mistakenly believe that they are already befriending the other when the image of the enemy suddenly reappears and turns that real person back into a stereotype. We need to understand that this step "backward" occurs as a result of an intrapsychic experience *during* the encounter with the other as a result of the kind of relational shock discussed earlier. Therefore, our challenge is to identify ways of finding the possibilities for *renewing* the relationship before it falls apart. In this kind of circular or at least nonlinear reading of events, we at Rondine keep coming back to the "during," to the crucial moment when renewal can occur.

In short, people are able to see that conflicts can be transformed if they come to trust one another and if they believe that the bonds between them can be strengthened over time, especially when they meet each other face-to-face. Jointly experiencing joy as well as pain during the two-year residency in Rondine can reduce the distance between them through collaborative interactions, whether work related or not, and in turn, allow them to share their deepest feelings with acquaintances who become true friends.

We have also learned that we cannot equate the terms "war" and "conflict" if we want to build sound relationships. In the next chapter, I will spend more time on why we should stop using the two terms as synonyms. The key here is to see that the heart of the matter for our purposes lies in the fact that conflict can change reality for the better, in part, because it can help us get beyond some of our most stubbornly held values. Here, it is useful to consider the Latin root of the word conflict. *Confligere* literally means to irritate. In that sense, how we deal with the friction that the irritation produces determines everything. It doesn't have to take a conflict in an aggressive or destructive direction. Conflict can also point us toward a positive, creative, and constructive path.

THE THREE LEVELS OF A RELATIONAL EXPERIENCE

The Rondine Method grows out of insights that we have reached over the last twenty years on three levels. As you will see, they start with concrete actions grounded in students' cognitive and social reality and then dig farther into their subconscious and more deeply held values.

The first deals with real behavior that is physical, direct, and immediate. It covers the ways people interact everywhere—at home, school, work, play, in conversation, and more, including texting and talking with each other on their phones and other devices. In this first interaction, there is no screen, only a face as in face-to-face encounters, as Levinas or Buber would see things.

The second level is in our subconscious and the ways it shapes our emotional reactions. As you know, we can think of the subconscious in many ways. For some, it is simply a catchall term for describing pain, as in Freud's notion that pain never disappears. For others, like Jung, the subconscious can also propel us forward. More recently, psychologists have come to think of it as a magma of thoughts and emotions that can be called to the surface through regular practice.

The third level is explicitly creative and occurs when two people commit to experiencing each other. That is when their images and dreams can influence each other at a particular place and time. This is the "space" in which they can explore their hopes and dreams while acknowledging their joint expectations. As a result, this third level always involves real-life situations as well as abstract discussions.

Together, the three levels allow people to achieve what we call "psychological accommodation." Operating on all three of them gives people something akin to a powerful lens that sharpens the way they see the world and brings the objects in it more clearly into focus. In that way, psychological accommodation becomes the concept through which subconscious thoughts and creative ideas can be transformed into concrete behavior for people on both sides of a divisive issue.

Psychological accommodation also ensures that the individual can shuttle across the three levels through what we call a process of self-adjustment. Rooted in reality, each individual can now become open to ongoing change without fear of becoming separated from the other. Because there is trust, the "lens" adjusts the psychological distance between people on both sides of a dispute. In psychological terms, it orients people toward a common target—strengthening their relationship.

I should add that the words "distance" and "separation" do not mean the same thing. The former is merely a measure of space, while the latter can only be understood through personal experience. Thus, we can feel a person who is physically close as being very far away. By contrast, we can be in what feels like intimate contact with a person who lives on a different and distant continent.

Operating on all three levels helps the individual find the sweet spot between closeness and intimacy on the one hand and separation and estrangement on the other, which defines what we think of as the relational experience. Psychological accommodation thus self-adjusts what can be thought of as the "near" and "far," both of which are in constant motion in ways that we cannot hope to measure (see Vaccari 2018a, 24).

This kind of truly shared experience opens the door to lasting change that goes beyond a vaguely conceived common future that resides solely in the mind of one of the participants. Through dialogue, cognitive skills allow people's creative potential to take center stage while minimizing the likelihood that either party will aggressively discredit the other and again distance themselves from each other.

When all is said and done, this is the conceptual turning point. Relational habits develop because two people use face-to-face interactions to share what had been private beliefs in what would have once been seen as risky encounters. Next we need to understand the paradox that underlies everything in this chapter. By taking risks in a stable environment, like the one we have created at Rondine, we can create the common or shared space that seems so elusive in today's digital world.

The Psychological Accommodation of Words, Images, and Emotions in the Relational Habitat

While it is helpful to use the image of a powerful lens in describing the psychological accommodation of words, images, and emotions, bringing something into focus does not always mean the same thing as shortening the distance between two objects. In psychological terms, there is no way we can shape the equivalent of a physical lens. It is more important to think metaphorically because a person can clearly see and interact meaningfully with the other who might physically be far away using phones, faxes, and other new technologies.

Our relational approach seeks to integrate experiences but not overcome dialectical and other deep differences. The psychological accommodation envisioned by Jung can be created in a supportive environment like Rondine's by strengthening the "us" without eliminating or even papering over the "I" and the "thou." That leads us to the definition of psychological accommodation as a unique product of the imagination in action that consolidates a relationship that could otherwise be blocked when painful memories resurface.

As in Gestalt theory, the "us" or "we" is placed at the center by (re)structuring the relationship itself. The individual moves into the background but not out beyond the edge, because each individual returns to the center of the psychological stage by closely paying attention to the words, perceptions, beliefs, and emotions of the other. We can all gain from practicing how psychological accommodation takes place because we can come up with new ways of connecting with one another through the interplay of fresh ideas and new experimental practices. This is one of the areas in our work in which recent discoveries by neuroscientists have been particularly helpful. Scientists no longer make a clear distinction between the roles played by the two hemispheres of the brain. That means that our minds are capable of:

> [f]orming mental images, of recombining them in a sort of continuous kaleidoscope inside of which both logical and imaginative associations take place. Imagination, based on grasping possible or impossible connections, implies vast knowledge and experience, even non-specific, since the broader they are, the higher the probability of perceiving relationships and consequently imagining solutions. (Oliverio 2013, 98–99)

THE FUNCTION OF FOCUSING ON THE OTHER PERSON'S LANGUAGE

We have seen relationships stabilize and grow when we can help individuals reach three end points through a series of dialogues:

- Discovering some common ground
- Accepting that differences exist between any two people let alone larger groups
- Acknowledging that there are limits to mutual understanding

A simple gesture might be enough to reach either of the first two. Areas of common ground and points of disagreement are both normal parts of everyday life that can easily coexist without compromising anyone's core identity. It is much harder to get to the third realization without also jumping to the conclusion that it is a negative, depressing, or even delusional outcome. Also, rationality won't help us here. Instead, we need a sensitivity to the other person's most intimate and cherished beliefs.

That leads to another question: Why is it so hard for people to call their cultural norms into question? Why does that lead to so much pain and strain? Students living at Rondine have asked us to answer these questions in ways that go far beyond their professional or political lives. To see what I am driving at here, consider these words from Maria, a former Armenian student at Rondine, who now serves as a member of her country's Parliament:

> If our words shape the world, our words also shape us. In my opinion, language defines and builds the world. This belief helped me tremendously when I started studying the transformation of conflicts,

and I started to deal with dialogue between people that are different.
(Vaccari and Simeoni 2019, 97)

Here, it is worth considering the difference between translating and understanding. If people truly want to respect others' worlds, they have to fully "tune in" to the others' language in all of its dimensions. That can even be the case between two people who live in the same culture and literally speak the same language. In fact, we all know that the word "language" is not simply a reflection of the individual words, phrases, or sentences an individual says aloud or commits to print. Language is an entirety that is learned in families and in other psychosocial environments.

Why then are understanding and translating from a foreign language not the same thing? The answer lies in the "fabric" that makes another tongue "foreign" and therefore "alien."

Everything from another language's syntax to the nuances its speakers convey to the way it is spoken can be disconcerting. They can evoke a wide variety of unconscious feelings and emotions, including stress and pain. At the same time, oral translations are always easier to make sense of than written ones because we can "hear" and "see" more of those emotions because we are sitting face-to-face with another person.

In other words, it is never possible for us to provide a truly faithful and literal translation of something another person says or does, especially when the writing is filled with what could be called connotative poetry. No matter how experienced a translator is, poetry and the like remain impossible to translate— at least in the literal sense of the term. The same applies to all dialogues, even among people who are at least superficially alike. Each person is unique when it comes to language, and in this sense, everyone's prose has a creative or poetic side that renders literal translation or complete understanding impossible.

Accepting this logic might seem to suggest that we can never truly understand another person, which can leave us unwilling and/or unable to interact with the other because what they see would seem incomprehensible on some important level. The ancient Greeks understood this when they coined an onomatopoeic word to use as the equivalent of the English word "barbarians" because they thought people who didn't speak their own language were simply uttering incomprehensible phrases like "ba, ba, ba."

As we see it at Rondine, acknowledging the limits of what we can hope to understand should not be confused with powerlessness. Wanting to start a relationship can help one discover the joys that can come from being connected to someone on the other, "dark," anxiety-inducing side of things because we can find ways of sharing common spaces and common moments, which, under the right circumstances, can lead to our renewal.

THE PERCEPTUAL ACCOMMODATION FUNCTION

If translating involves processing everything and not just the spoken or written word, understanding calls on what I earlier called psychological adjustment in which we use our two eyes to balance the three levels at which we have to engage—the concrete, the unconscious, and the creative. That balancing act reaches its peak when we are able to reach a Zen-like detachment and our real vision of the other begins to come together. At that point, our in-depth understanding also becomes a forward-looking one in which we "adjust" the mental distance between ourselves and the other.

We all have had firsthand experience of the gap between the real and the subconscious. How often have we heard simple and not very worrisome statements like "I was listening to what he was saying, but it took me a while to figure out what he was thinking"? On the other hand, there are also times when the subconscious content overwhelms us to the point that we can't tell where a daydream ends and reality begins. Our students, for example, follow some idle thoughts and end up mentally drifting out of the classroom while still looking at the teacher, not realizing that they have wandered onto what amounts to a different planet.

The same thing happens at professional conferences. A presentation might start off being interesting but soon becomes hard to follow once it sparks and then interrupts an internal "dialogue with ourselves." By contrast, in a real human interaction with another person, the alternation between people talking makes a creative exchange possible.

Those discussions can then take on a serious tone. For example, while focusing on trying to understand, rather than simply translating the other, a speaker can make progress by stopping and asking their partner a simple question like "Are you following me?" when their body language suggests that they are confused or not paying attention. Once those distortions occur, our insights can become so blurry that they lead us to make mistakes because we lose the ability to see all the contours in what they are trying to tell us. It is as if we are being blinded by the sun while walking on a glacier in the middle of winter. It is at such a time that we need our powerful mental lens to provide the psychological adjustment that allows us to clearly see both things that are near at hand and things that are physically or emotionally far away.

In that kind of "near–far" practice, we are likely to develop some discomfort. That's why we always have to pay attention to and maintain the relationship so that we can see clearly and productively into the future, a point we will return to in the next chapter.

The Final Opening: Nurturing Emotional Intelligence

It is always a good idea to compare your own interpretations with those of people you disagree with because doing so allows you to bring those subconscious values and beliefs into the open. In that respect, I surprisingly found myself in agreement with the well-known American philosopher Martha Nussbaum (2001), who has been exploring the relationship between what she calls upheavals of thought and emotional intelligence for the last twenty years or more. Because her title, *The Upheavals of Thought*, makes sense, I find it useful to paraphrase and add on to her words the idea that our thoughts and ethical judgments are invariably shaped by our emotions. Upheavals of thought can also be thought of as having effects comparable to the jolting shocks of an earthquake, as the English term *upheaval* implies. Emotions such as pain, fear, shame, love, and *compassion* are an integral part of a philosophy pervaded by the *pathos* of knowledge, as has been the case throughout recorded history.

From her perspective, emotions can be seen as appraisals or value judgments, which can have a huge impact on our well-being. Like many of the others on whom Rondine's work is based, Nussbaum focuses on the formative years when each child or adolescent has to figure out their own limitation and, therefore, dependence on the other.

Like Winnicott, Nussbaum agrees that emotions are a lens through which we interpret our cultural norms and much more. We can see that in the ways that the arts stimulate creativity in all realms and can make our shared space one in which we can all grow. And that takes us back to the entire life cycle since, as she suggests, an adult's emotions cannot be understood without first understanding their childhood or adolescence.

Given what we've seen so far, psychological adjustment must seem like an abstract concept. We will, however, turn to how it can be put to practical use in the next chapter.

Note

1. Late in life, Jung made the case that while every aspect of reality is understood through psychological mechanisms, not everything can be explained solely through the use of psychological dynamics. For more, see Morelli (2019, 39).

CHAPTER 4

Putting the Relational Model to the Test

Franco Vaccari

As I noted at the end of chapter 2, our theoretical model has two uses—to explain shock and trauma that inhibits the interactions between two former enemies and to outline the kind of transformative changes their relationship could lead to. What you just saw in chapter 3 makes the case that changing the nature of their relationship could make a huge difference. That hypothesis, however, must be tested. As we have put it into practice, the Rondine Method helps young people who have been victimized by war and conflict overcome their past and, especially, the trauma that comes with it. That is why it is so important to think of Rondine as a lab or workshop where we constantly develop and refine these ideas.

A Positive Approach to Conflict

Our model posits that everything that takes place in a relationship can lead to friction and that any time that "something goes wrong," we are faced with a challenge that we need to address. It may be tempting to sweep those challenges under the rug under the illusion that the people involved think that they already understand each other well enough.

However, if the parties do not explore their concrete differences because they are afraid of what they might discover or what might happen, they can fall into a vicious cycle in which the entire relationship falls apart. As it deteriorates, we increasingly see the others as a serious threat whether they are or not. Our nightmares will deepen until we are overwhelmed by pain and anguish, which cannot fully be diagnosed as a result of whatever general psychological problems we might have.

The relationship continues falling down the metaphorical staircase especially if an external event makes matters worse. In time, the prejudices and stereotypes get blended into the way the parties think about the very conflict itself. A lively discussion can turn into a heated dispute because the parties assume that they are "making war" with each other. That takes us to the point that instead of dealing with a simple dispute or disagreement, we find ourselves in the equivalent of a counterproductive and all-out war. The relationship breaks down, taking with it any trust they might have in what an extended dialogue could produce in terms of reaching common understandings about the dispute itself.

Thus, it is clear to us that a positive approach to conflict has to combine a search for common ground as well as an analysis of our differences and our frictions. In that sense, it is vitally important that we see how a shift in the language we use and the stories we tell can make more sweeping change possible as we saw at a theoretical level in chapter 3.

A LINGUISTIC SHIFT: CONFLICT IS NOT WAR

The military undoubtedly gave the term *conflict* its negative connation—battle, struggle between states, war, and the like. However, since ancient times, we have also had a more expansive view of what causes hostility—deep disagreements about ideas, interests, and feelings. Conflict in that sense of the term does not necessarily lead to violence and/or destruction; it also does not imply that "enemies" exist everywhere we turn. Often, however, the word *conflict* does conjure up negative connotations, and its polarizing implications get overblown. Among other things, we should do some research into the evolution of the major Indo-European and Middle Eastern languages so that we can find how the original meaning of the word got lost. That, of course, would take us way beyond the scope of this book.

Over the years, any number of philosophers and social scientists have concluded that conflict has negative implications when it evokes open hostility and the intentional desire to harm other people from whom one has to defend oneself, whether seen in terms of individuals or groups. They go on to argue that our ancestors created the state and other forms of government because they could protect us from crime, violence, and the like. Thus, during the centuries when the first civilizations emerged in the Tigris River valley, religious organizations and ethical codes turned war into a sacred way of protecting ourselves from threats, whether they came from inside a given society or arose beyond its borders.

To be sure, we do need something like a legal code that defines certain acts as unacceptable or illegal. That does not justify, however, equating conflict with violence and war and the obsessive belief that some "evil villain" lives on our doorstep. But it does help us understand the social dynamics that feed mistrust in our fellow humans and in the fact that so many of us try to avoid conflict whenever possible.

It is easy to forget the fact that humans have survived and overcome conflict in most areas of our lives—with friends and family, political opponents, coworkers, and even people of other faiths. We also tend to forget how often those conflicts evoked deeply held, negative emotions. Along the way, we can lose sight of the fact that we can manage our differences by, for instance, competing on the athletic field rather than in do-or-die disputes with our enemies.

Therefore, it is hardly surprising that we have reframed the way we speak about conflict to the point that we mistakenly assume that those who "stand in our way" always pose some sort of existential threat. By that logic, anything like renewal has to start with a vision or worldview that builds trust between people who disagree with each other, which shifts us away from the prejudice that leads us to the conclusion that our differences can't be reconciled, such as "I-don't-want-to have-anything-to-do-with-this-other-person" and "they-are-too-different-from us."

CULTURAL PROFILE

The cultural project that "redeems" the idea of conflict from those negative connotations has to help individuals take several painful steps and adopt a different mindset about how we could or should deal with our disputes. When a dispute leads to traumatic experiences, that redemption is hard to reach because of the way any conflict tests our self-awareness and self-confidence. The choices we make—loyalty, determination, tenacity, integrity, and more—reflect our values as they spring up from the everyday realities of a given crisis and the suffering it leads to. Our cultural profiles start with distant, abstract, and oftentimes falsely constructed ideas about ourselves and others, all of which carry more immediate connections to our lived experiences.

I have been thinking along these lines for a long time. As early as 1976 when I was writing my PhD thesis with Ernesto Valentini, who was a Jesuit priest as well as a clinical psychologist, I had already homed in on the idea of homeostasis or a system's stability. Biologists had been using the term since 1929 when Walter Cannon (who also seems to have invented the phrase "flight or fight") started using it to describe the human body's physical dynamics. I was convinced that it could also be used in dealing with psychodynamic systems.

Since then, many more analysts have used homeostasis—or the lack thereof—in understanding a wider variety of social dynamics, including conflict. They have added other ideas to the list, including entropy (in which a system deteriorates), allostasis (in which a system returns to a stable state), and even heterostasis (in which a system remains stable across multiple, overlapping, and often contradictory dimensions). All three help us see that a complex but stable system is also constantly in motion (Sterling and Eyer 1988). Allostasis (which is sometimes referred to as the creation of a eufunctional or growing system) is a particularly important concept for our purposes because it helps us see how any individual, group, or society can constructively respond to an emergency by pointing to how neural regulatory systems help us adapt to a continually changing environment.

Research findings suggest that conflict between the cells in our bodies is a defining characteristic of life itself because it, too, involves coming to grips with difference. Each movement toward growth and stability comes with a cost—the use of force in physics, reactions in biochemistry, and interplay of unconscious psychological dynamics. Sometimes these costs can seem neutral in that they contribute neither to a system's growth nor decay. In the kinds of human relationships we are interested in here, the emotional cost can be substantial and may be hard to calculate in the short term because the efforts themselves have their roots in our subconscious.

As a child, every human being learns about social roles and rules at home, at school, and beyond. Growing up involves risk-taking as children explore the conflicting stimuli and demands they confront. Learning how to deal with conflict is a kind of final exam in that educational process through which we demonstrate how much we have learned about social dynamics. Thus, conflict is a bit like rock climbing in which the critical thresholds of dealing with the self, solitude (but not isolation), and freedom represent the "peaks."

Chronologically, the stages of life follow each other—from the silent fetus to the screaming baby, from nursing to weaning, from the family at home to the first days at kindergarten and elementary school, from toys to adolescence, and from parenting to old age. At each of these stages, new relationships open up and close down "horizontally." Some of them just fade into memories, while a few last a lifetime because they are constantly redefined and bring regular new beginnings and endings as well as moments when we make significant new connections and end up being abandoned.

Thus, conflict is a natural outgrowth of the tensions among the multiple facets or aspects of our lives. As Manuel Benasayag and Angélique del Rey put it:

> [e]verything is governed by conflict, and whenever someone tries to ignore its existence, the conflict only precipitates men and women into the vortex of the unreal. However, embracing the conflict, far from endorsing the need for confrontation, affirms the very principle of creating the new. (Benasayag and Del Rey 2008, 204)

Indifference toward conflict lays the groundwork for a more violent confrontation because it allows the unconscious part of the "us versus them" mentality to fester. Seeing the world in terms of inevitably conflicting polarization leads to the contempt for others, which I have already discussed. As the late Israeli writer Amos Oz liked to put it, statements like "if there were no enemies, we would have to invent them" feeds into the perverse logic of prejudice against the other.

Here, our thinking differs from Johan Galtung's (2004) critical contributions on "transcending" and "transforming" conflicts. He thinks we can end polarization altogether as reflected in the countless mediation experiments and other interventions to eradicate what he calls "structural violence." If we are right, it is trauma and the other phenomena we focus on that prevent a person or group from living a life that is worth living. As a result, Galtung and others who have designed effective negotiating models, which have been used around the world, have not gone far enough in determining how we can also change those core emotions, beliefs, and values along the way.

This is exactly what we have tried to do in the research we have conducted to test the Rondine Method. Slowly but surely, youthful former enemies come to understand that conflict can be a good thing by learning how to identify and accept the similarities and differences that grow out of the kinds of frictions I have discussed so far in this book.

> This occurs when—according to the Hewstone and Brown model—the encounter and contact with the "enemy" become the encounter with a person with whom I recognize a common humanity but at the same time our differences, a person who maintains his identity as I keep mine. (Iafrate and Bertoni 2019, 122)

All these scholars and practitioners have made important, but partial, contributions to the kinds of conflicts we address at Rondine. What we have tried to do is to put forward our own point of view, which stresses the positive side of conflict, something that can be achieved by rekindling mutual trust, which can be the first step toward opening to a productive life with the other. As Luca Alici (2012) put it:

> [w]e are all dependent on something that is bigger and outside of ourselves. Trust can represent the ground on which to experiment, a model of rationality able to exist with vulnerability and fragility, and discern, in the multiple types of bonds that characterize our existence, the conditions for talking about healthy or pathological dependence. Fragile and perishable, but not suppressible, trust is an essential relational asset, which attests and circumscribes the presence of constitutive openness, even within our most intimate dynamics. (53)

Creating the Enemy: From Mirage to Distortion to Ghosts

What happens at that moment when an existing relationship ends and gives way to the creation of an enemy? If we let our fear of engaging them overwhelm us, any contact becomes riskier and risker and whatever trust used to exist between us will disappear until we reach the bottom when any kind of constructive contact seems out of the question. At that point, the ways we project our fear onto the "face" of the other leads us to conjure up misleading images and engage in distorted communications, which end up turning the other into what amounts to devils and illusions, whom we invent ourselves.

THE PSYCHOTIC MIRAGE AND FAILED RELATIONSHIPS

I find it helpful to use terms from optics to explain psychological phenomena. In this case, I often use the Italian word *miraggio*, which carries more dire implications than its closest English equivalent, *mirage*. In the kinds of conflicts we work on at Rondine, we find that people typically distort the way they view the other in human conflict to the point that they see it, instead, in the hazy, ill-defined, and misleading ways that the word *mirage* conveys. Once that happens, one shouldn't be surprised that discussions involving both sides degenerate into sterile self-justifications and polemics while any hope of sharing real desires tends to fly out the metaphorical window.

To see what I'm driving at, consider these paragraphs from the Treccani dictionary, Italy's equivalent of Wikipedia:

> A mirage is an atmospheric optical phenomenon caused by the deviation that light rays undergo because of the refractions and reflections they are subjected to when they cross adjacent layers of air, characterized by different temperatures and densities and therefore by a different refractive index.
>
> By extension, the word indicates the appearance of non-existent objects that don't really exist, due to particular atmospheric conditions or states of hallucination, physical malaise, psychological disturbance: a desert oasis or an island in the middle of the ocean.

A psychological mirage "appears" when people begin distorting the images they have of themselves and of each other. If they each see a mirage (and the two will almost certainly not be the same), they can no longer keep their fears and anxiety under control. They see each other as threats. But as often as not, the images in the mirages are not real, or if they do represent real phenomena, they are distorted in such a way that neither party can react constructively. It also becomes easy to decide that the safest thing to do is to avoid all contact with the other side.

But why is this so worrisome? When two people who are in a fluctuating or combustible relationship cease being able to see a good side to their disagreements, they become subject to radical or polarizing appeals, emotional blackmail, and the like. They no longer face each other in any kind of meaningful way and may not speak with or listen to the other person at all. Any closeness between them disappears. Under better circumstances, they might have said things like "I feel bad because I don't understand you" "Are you upset?" or "What happened to you?" Now, those kinds of questions are reserved for "friends" in one's in-group. Everyone else becomes "them," or the enemy.

In time, the relationship deteriorates until it collapses altogether. Terms like *deception* and *mirage* get used interchangeably because the two individuals or groups have drifted so far apart. To borrow a term from physics, the relationship has gone through a phase transition in the way that water does when it freezes or boils. In this case, instead of turning into ice or steam, the feelings turn toxic. This is what Martha Nussbaum (2001) had in mind when she argued that intense anger can morph into hatred and an attempt to mortify or even eliminate the other.

Most observers would point to two possible outcomes once things have gotten to this point. First, people could acknowledge their differences and decide to "peacefully end the relationship." Second (and more tragically), they could drag each into their respective mirages and magnify the distortions and prejudices they already have about each other. When this happens, people steadily turn toward deceit—and worse. We call this a "deceptive switch," which has a lot in common with what happens when dissociative identity disorders present themselves in patients with multiple personalities whose anxiety is so intense that they have no hope of unifying them into a single coherent whole (Lingiardi 2019, 35–38).

Therein lies the ability to move across the three levels of communication that I talked about in chapter 3—actual behavior, the unconscious, and the activity of the imagination—from which violence rises to the surface, even if it isn't all that destructive at first.

THE "TRUE" CREATION OF THE FABRICATED ENEMY

In what amounts to a second stage, there is an upheaval in which the individual creates an enemy by transforming the kind of defensive or aggressive distortion of the other person's real nature into what I just described as a mirage, a stereotype, and a self-constructed illusion. Oddly enough, the mirage now seems like an all too real flesh-and-bones enemy whom you can defend yourself against, fight, and eliminate.

Once that psychological transition or synthesis has occurred, the idea of a relational shock, as discussed in chapters 1 and 2, comes into play because the mirage can now easily slip into destructive action. Depending on the circumstances, one person (or both) can fall prey to an emotional short circuit in which the meaning of every emotion, thought, or behavior that comes from the other gets blown out of proportion. The person now focuses on keeping the other at bay, excluding or eliminating them under the illusion that there are no "others" who could step between them and improve the situation. Meanwhile, given the nature of the mirage and the fears it produces, it appears as if the world truly consists of only "us" versus "them."

"Misdirecting" actions invariably follow. The two people think they are interacting with each other, but, in reality, they are surrounded by other figures in their social and relational history who fan the flames. It is as if the pace of history sped up as each side (mis)remembers the past and ends up hiding the other's true "face." The other person is now seen as nothing more than an enemy because they "obviously" are responsible for all the pain and suffering. Whatever happens between the two sides turns into a bevy of attacks and counterattacks, with each side accusing the other of every crime imaginable.

We fabricate these false selves, "mirages," or "enemies," so that we can justify our decision to avoid relating to others in one of two ways. We can passively tune them out by simply ignoring them and telling ourselves that "I already know what they are like, so there's no need to talk with them anymore." We can also do so by actively putting them down or, in the most pathological cases, attacking and even killing them. In that kind of situation, defensive projection takes over, and we unleash a tirade of angry words, our face hardens, a kind of homicidal denial consumes us, and we utter phrases like "I don't want to have anything to do with that person ever again."

When people are exposed to what they perceive to be threatening stimuli, reactive experiences like anger and hatred blend with the legacy of long-standing

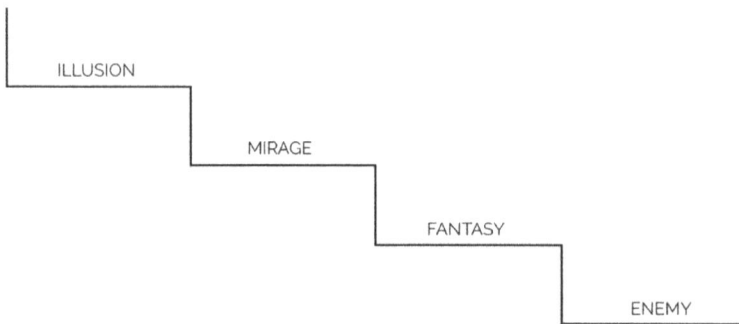

Figure 4.1.   The Enemy Staircase: Illusion, Mirage, Fantasy, Enemy

traumatic experiences. These adverse by-products of a person's relational history build a psychological wall of defiance, which, like a physical barrier, can withstand all kinds of pressure without cracking. In a sense, a person's hardened face serves as a metaphor for the general short-circuiting that such a barrier creates as depicted in figure 4.1.

One no longer sees a real face. The fabricated face of the other has replaced the real human being.

Deconstructing the Enemy

We can "deconstruct" the image of the enemy by prioritizing a healthy relationship, which is the point at which the Rondine Method is put to the test. When faced with a relational shock, an individual can find the courage to reach out to an enemy across their shared pain and find the empowering energy that emerges when people truly meet across their differences.

As figure 4.2 and the rest of this section suggest, talking about their shared pain is the turning point that takes place as people "climb the steps" up the mental "staircase." The hurt and suffering no longer bursts out just like blood does from a gaping wound and, instead, turns into strands of yarn through which a dialogue with the other can be woven. Constructive dialogue leads to breakthroughs that erase the enemy's ghostlike scaffolding. That psychological and generative relational bridge allows the individual to (re)engage in constructive relationships despite the distorted images and the like, which have created so many problems in the past.

As that happens, they come to realize that creating such a psychological bridge not only removes the barriers that prevent "real" communication between them but also creates a new "relational space," which helps them go up the staircase. We have identified this twofold sequence of transforming shared suffering by carefully observing the young people who come to live at the World House.

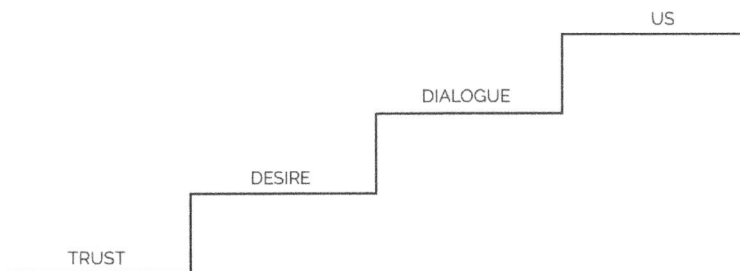

Figure 4.2.   The Stairs Going Up: Trust, Desire, Dialogue, and "Getting to Us"

DISCOVERING A SUFFERING PERSON IN THE ENEMY BEYOND THE FIREWALL

Once the situation becomes unbearable, the individual has to find their own way out. They have to search for the "key that unlocks the door" in the one place where they had never previously sought to look—in face-to-face encounters with the other.

That starts with (re)establishing trust through a mediator or other third party with whom an individual can "break through" the firewall and unblock the stalemate. In their ongoing work with the Rondine staff, the students identify areas of hatred that they were not even aware of that had surfaced as a result of a particular relational shock. For example, Ibrahim from Palestine "understood that my conflict with my enemy was the fear I carried in my heart," or in El-mira from Azerbaijan's words, "We grew up with pain in our souls, under the propaganda of hatred towards the enemy and perhaps we had the right to hate them." Her fellow Azerbaijani Maria said something similar: "There is usually a personal reason why we allow hatred to arise within us: it is that we find this difficult to admit."

To see how the ghostlike constructions get in the way of working relationships, consider what the Palestinian Issa had to say about what he and Rotem, a young Israeli woman, did to turn away from what amounted to a raging stream of unconscious anger and hatred.

> In those first weeks when the war in Gaza resumed, we started, Rotem and I, to discuss the situation, and I was struck by the fact that we were talking about the same city that has two different names, we were talking about the same event about which we had different stories. We argued a lot, and we rarely agreed. As soon as something happened in our land, emotions came into play and took us to other discussion levels, but then we set rules and *followed* them. Whenever I talked to Rotem, we got closer. And I started to feel that the trust I lacked at the beginning, at some point comes out, it exists.

Issa's statement tells us a lot. At Rondine, we focus on those kinds of tools that allow the young people to manage their hostility enough to stop "creating" the enemy. These two young people from the Middle East learned how to leave their prejudices behind. A very different and "real" person emerged. As he went on to say, "emotions came into play and led us to other levels of discussion, but then we set ground rules, and we followed them."

Because they can talk about their pain, the young people at Rondine are able to engage with each other. They can use one of their "eyes" to look inside their own mirage and its ghostlike images while the second "eye" can explore the reality of the other's life and (re)connect with their lived experiences. Psychological accommodation begins to take place anew. They can have civil discussions and arguments. They can set ground rules so that they don't get overwhelmed by the specter of polarization. Needless to say, there can still be a huge emotional distance between them, but their emerging trust lets them get beyond simplistic assertions that one or the other of them is totally right while the one is always wrong.

In a very real sense, this realization leads to a paradox that an Israeli student at Rondine, Noam, pointed out in a conversation we had a few years ago:

> The only person who understands me is my enemy, because being my counterpart in the conflict, he has lived through what I have lived through, but from the other side. In a situation of enmity between two peoples the pressure is highly conditioning. The enemy's presence also determines the development of each one's identity, therefore, the "poisoned identity" Franco Vaccari always talks about—the need for purification. After all, he is a bit right when he jokingly says that Rondine has a homeopathic approach to conflict. It is not because of the little progress and few daily changes we make, but it is the choice to heal the illness with diluted, infinitesimal doses of the poison producing it. The enemy in person is placed next to who wants to exit the enemy's ghost. (Vaccari and Simeoni 2019, 65)

In the words of Cardinal Carlo Maria Martini, who was Archbishop of Milan from 1979 to 2003, there is another reason to look for a way of acknowledging the other's pain. After he retired, he moved to Jerusalem, where he fought a long battle with a terminal illness. Shortly before he died in August 2009, he included these words in a letter he sent to the residents of his adoptive city as his disease worsened.

> If people only look at their own pain, resentment, reprisal, and revenge will always prevail. However, if the memory of pain will also lead to remembering that the other is suffering, too, interacting with the stranger, and even the enemy can represent the beginning of understanding. Voicing the pain of others is the premise of any future peace policy. (Vaccari 2018b, 149)

CROSSING THE BRIDGE OF RENEWAL

At this point, the students at Rondine have reached what we call the "bridge of renewal," where they can each take the first "step" toward each other from their respective sides of the "water."

A single incident shows how absurd the situation becomes when someone's pain can't be put into words, even when the people involved think they want to talk to one another. Kameliah—a young Palestinian woman—was on the verge of a nervous breakdown during one of the periods when Israeli forces were attacking occupied Palestinian Territories. She wanted to move beyond her anger, pain, and suffering, but days passed without anything happening. When I suggested, "Why don't you talk to Guy [the Israeli student] about it?" her answer appeared like a bolt out of the blue. "I can't; he is suffering so much, and he wouldn't be able to stand it if we added my pain too."

It can feel like a nightmare when the fear that no one can penetrate your pain reappears. Luckily, the memory that there is someone else with whom you have been working for some time and who isn't like the others in the enemy group can reappear too. Together, two persons can chip away at the firewall that stands between them and explore each other's strengths and talents in the process of overcoming relational barriers.

In restarting the relationship with the former enemy, the two people recognize each other as whole people once again and re-create the space in which they can interact constructively. It is only at this point that they can resolve the paradox in ways that Guy understood. "My enemy's heart is the promised land." His fellow Israeli, Yahel, echoed those thoughts. "It went down into my emotional bunker because I was worried about the safety of my loved ones. Then, for the first time, I began worrying about my former enemies. 'Where is Rabi? Where is he?'" In that way, some young Palestinians were protected in the (emotional) homes of some young Israelis during those incredibly tough times in 2014.

If you want to walk across the bridge of renewal, you have to be open to genuine dialogue. If those dialogues are going to happen, we have to bring all of our humanity to the table and be willing to talk about our pain with all of the words, silences, and stares that come with it. No magical tools are needed to facilitate those discussions because people who truly share the same space and time find the new words that they need on their own, even if there is a lot of stammering and stuttering along the way. Dialogue participants become aware that what the other person says has to be understood as a matter of trust.

During this second stage, the Rondine staff members slip into the background. The relationship between the former enemies is strong enough to take center stage on its own because the young people have rediscovered their lost joint humanity. Although a mediator may be needed to get the ball rolling again, the students can now pretty much continue forward on their own. Here, think about what Elmira, from Armenia, had to say:

> The hatred of that first meeting is gone, now it is over. At least between the two of us, it's over. And I will always remember that when I saw you the first time, I didn't want to shake your hand; when I

said goodbye to you for the *last* time, I chose to hug you. But how is all this possible?

Her joy and amazement demonstrate once and for all that she has crossed the bridge that has renewed her capacity to relate to her perceived enemy.

It might have seemed impossible at first. Still, the fact is that people can make the deceptive, dangerous, and damaging mirage disappear by meeting those they think of as their enemies and listening to their anger, pain, and sorrow. When two or more individuals get to the point where they can see themselves as victims of each other's failures and prejudices, they can embrace new perspectives that are 180 degrees different from the ones they started with.

People in Relationship Know How to Share Pain

You have just seen some of the ways the young people who have spent time at Rondine have changed because of their willingness to deconstruct the enemy through discussions with members of our staff and with each other.

Young people have learned how to restore relationships by expressing their pain especially once they have to "rediscover" it either because of an unexpected relational shock or in the normal course of our discussions at Rondine. It is never easy to talk about one's reactions to traumatic events. And we can't guarantee that they will continue to understand that pain in the same light once they return to their own country and its history of violence and conflict.

Bearing in mind the importance of stabilizing relationships amid conflict, we can close the circle on the Rondine Method by seeing how it combines theory and practice. Because we have tried to make sense of the twenty years' worth of work using Rondine's educational/training model, we have been able to develop what we have come to call the *relational theory for transforming intractable conflicts*.

So the missing final step involves truly coming to grips with pain until it can provide the student with what might be thought of as a "relational surplus," which helps keep mutual trust alive even when the relationship itself hits major bumps in the road in two key ways. First, we help students learn how to manage conflict by exploring their similarities and differences while avoiding those dangerous images of the enemy. The second one helps give people the ability to deal with suffering and avoid the suffering that so often accompanies traumatic events.

GIVING WORDS TO PAIN

> *Give sorrow words; the grief that does not speak knits up the*
> *o-er wrought heart and bids it break.*

—Shakespeare, *Macbeth*, act IV, scene III

One of the most famous lines from Macbeth also resonates in various parts of the world when we stage *Dissonanze in Accordo* (*Dissonance in Agreement*), which is a "nonshow show" we use to spread the word about Rondine. Among other things, the young people tell their personal stories and bear witness to how they have overcome the pain induced by the kinds of relational shocks I have described throughout part 1 of this book.

To see that, consider one final statement from one of our former students who has learned how to put her pain into words, words that helped her move forward.

> At Rondine, they do not teach us to give up our identity. Quite the opposite. When you start talking about the pain that conflict causes to you while listening to the others, you cannot double down on your own identity; if you do, you will end up offending the other person's feelings. Then everything begins to change: our pain is the same as the other's. In the past, we could not see it because we had grown up under the propaganda of hatred towards the enemy. I came to Rondine to listen to my enemy's pain, but, when on some occasions, the other person is already feeling terrible, we must respect him/her in silence.
>
> After comparing our situations, especially when we return to Rondine for the Rondine International Peace Lab meetings, we realized that pain is not generic in our countries. It is a specific kind of pain, which we experience after having suffered an injustice. Furthermore, this kind of pain, as Franco always says, does not evaporate!

That's why the idea of relational shocks, which I introduced in chapter 3, is so important. They produce the kinds of mental short circuits that lead any of us to not just view the other as the enemy but also as the one who was responsible for creating the conflict in the first place. Because "they" caused the problem, we place all of the blame on them for starting the conflict and all of the anguish it produced. That's why we have placed so much emphasis on discussing that pain and trauma in face-to-face relationships so that it can become the "go-to place" where we can begin reuniting the unconscious with reality.

When and if that happens, the emotional aftermath of the pain and trauma war leaves in its wake can be turned into a kind of "renewable energy" that nurtures the creative conflict transformation. Rondine's innovative path across the relational bridge can reverse the pain because it can redirect all of the wasted or spent energies it produces. After all, it is what we need to successfully navigate the world because it improves how we "metabolize" the events that shape our lives. When crossing the bridge, we convert the pain into mental "ashes" that we leave on one end and convert into constructive energy for growth, which keeps us moving toward the other side. When that happens, we don't forget the ashes, but they no longer can poison our memories or inhibit our actions. Put simply, we can't deal with trauma in this way unless we first accept the realities of the conflict head-on.

Confronting pain is not easy. It is, however, the price we pay for human recovery from the kinds of emotional wounds that bring people to places like Rondine. Paying that price allows us to process or "metabolize" the pain and limit its impact on us. It turns suffering into something like a pale pastel color in which we can recall what happened but not let these memories poison what we do today. This is something that the psychiatrist Victor Frankl (1962) so eloquently wrote about in his memoir about life in a Nazi concentration camp. The title given to the book when it was reprinted in 1962, *Man's Search for Meaning*, suggests that the deepest trauma and suffering can be turned into amazing opportunities for growth. As a founder of what became existential psychiatry, Frankl was among the first to see that opening up about the kind of pain and suffering he experienced can be the only way to survive in the short run and thrive into the future.

GIVING MEANING TO SUFFERING

We have no choice but to protect ourselves from pain. The evolutionary success of our species was only possible because of it. For about 200,000 years, *homo sapiens sapiens* has learned that pain leads to death and that, therefore, we do everything to avoid it and to fight everything that creates it. In this sense, pain, which is at the heart of any intractable conflict, also has to be part of any attempt to overcome it.

It is easy to see our ambivalent attitude toward pain in the psychological dynamics that lead us to be wary of discussing the toll that intractable conflict takes with others even when traumatic events are not involved. It's never logical or rational. But when it appears, it damages the way we view and interact with others.

In the short run, we might be able to get away with not acknowledging these effects. However, once we end up at the edge of an emotional precipice, it contributes both to our own trauma and to that of other people. Both become tone deaf. The other person, we believe, is incapable of understanding me, while we begin doubting everything up to and including our own sanity. If it goes on for too long, pain and suffering take over the relationship as we have already seen.

When people choose to cross the bridge of renewal, two gateways emerge—one at each end. Each person can proceed with the other's permission and support. They each make the decision to start because they embrace the idea of crossing into the other's "border" while being open to leaving their own. That's true because they have shown the desire to live beyond each of their borders: "I exit from my world in order to enter into yours." If they don't, they will end up strengthening the mirage and hastening the destruction that "ghost enemies" can cause.

In normal relationships, people move in and out of their comfort zones. They try out new ideas and experiences and take what they've learned back to their "home base." But it is in that "no-man's land," in the middle, that real change can occur. We have been trying to create that kind of dynamic for the people who come to Rondine since we created the World House more than twenty years ago. Even if there is no precise word that exists in either English or Italian to capture this interstitial space, what we have been trying to create is a space of "co-relationships," or reciprocity.

Once again, borrowing a phrase from another language can help. In this case, the closest German equivalent of reciprocity, or co-relationship, is *gegen-seitigkeit*, which literally means being in harmony. It is thus a concept:

> [T]hat manages to contain the need for change in those who live the reality of reciprocity, so much so that the term can be rendered as follows. "I am no longer what I was before I met you; you are no longer what you were before you met me." (Galantino 2018, 118)

CHAPTER 5

Some Final Thoughts and Next Steps

Franco Vaccari

The Rondine Method now has a demonstrated track record when it comes to creative conflict transformation (Vaccari 2018a, 2018b). Nonetheless, it is still a work in progress in two ways, which I would like to touch on in ending this overview.

The "Microcredit" of Relational Trust

First, we continue the work we have done over the last ten to twenty years in what amounts to using a psychotherapeutic and educational approach to working with young adults at the World House. All of our projects focus on creating relations that are based on what we now refer to as a "permanent home for trust." We also have begun to think of our work as a psychological equivalent of microcredit. As Nobel Prize–winning economist Muhammad Yunus and others have shown, very small loans made to poor women who use the money to start businesses can set off economic chain reactions that lift families and entire communities out of abject poverty. It is our belief that permanent habits of trust can set off similar chain reactions in people's minds.

We believe that developing a home for trust must be at the heart of any effort to remake the world for the better for two overlapping reasons that have been at the heart of everything I've written about in the previous four chapters.

First, we are convinced that interpersonal trust is a kind of new dimension that "guarantees space for *mutual recognition*" (Lingiardi 2019, 72), based on the idea developed by Benjamin (2017). Second, we have also learned that any such space can be made more solid and permanent in ways that make conflict transformation possible because of face-to-face exchanges between two people in which they:

- Demonstrate a willingness to change themselves
- Become open to sharing their pain with others

Taken together, these two points open the door to a useful paradox. A relationship can reach the kind of stabilization I talked about in chapter 4 only if it becomes a space that nurtures interactions between the parties that keeps both sides open to change in the following ways.

Shared memory can take hold only when all participants in the relationship are willing adopt a new identity that deepens as their interactions develop, as suggested by the likes of Erik Erikson. In their reconciled relationship, past and present coexist in ways that lead people to be optimistic about the future. It means paying more attention to the *inter* in interrelationship, which also leads to giving time itself a new meaning. This is also why I will keep emphasizing the word *fragment* in the rest of my contribution to this book. Given what we have learned from Martin Buber, Emmanuel Levinas, and Carl Jung, we have to be engaged in a nonstop exercise in which we (re)define who we are in light of the other so that we can imagine the future together.

As Viktor Frankl taught us more than half a century ago, both parties in a relationship can discover the essence of pain together, especially when the wound each of them suffers cuts deep. As we saw in chapter 4, we can unleash our imagination's transformational force, become open to new ideas, and foster compassion if we can escape the fear brought on by constant pain. Whether one is speaking Italian or English, the word *compassion* can be hard to define precisely. Unlike the Greek word *sympatheia*, from which it is derived, compassion calls on us to both pay attention to and respect the other, especially in hard times. In other words, a long line of thinkers from Jung to Winnicott to Weil have helped us see that being compassionate toward others literally means to be passionate with them, especially when they are in deep trouble.

To borrow a metaphor from the world of information technology, it helps to think of any healthy relationship as a "trust portal." The interchange best takes place when it is integrated into the relational hardware, which allows a supportive set of memories to form. At that point, the participants can then exchange their feelings of trauma and pain by using the equivalent of software, which is what we help them learn at Rondine.

Taking these points together, our work has convinced us that full human renewal occurs through strong interpersonal relationships between and among former enemies. Indeed, they have gotten so strong that people on both sides can practically "channel" what the person on the other side thinks and feels.

When we coined the phrase "a permanent home for trust," we wanted to emphasize the connection between space and time as a two-part experience in ways that an anthropologist would understand.

On the one hand, we wanted to safeguard diversity among human beings in one key way. If we can promote everybody's dignity, each person can begin to develop positive feelings toward the other. Those feelings can involve just about anything because they can span generations, social and ethnic groups, and nationalities and do so under the most challenging circumstances when it otherwise would be impossible to manage distortions, hostility, and hatred, which so often lead to disaster.

On the other hand, creating a permanent home for trust can help people overcome the main barriers that often prevent us from transforming intractable conflicts and achieving anything resembling human renewal, which stems from all but the total inability to communicate across lines of division. These include victimization, dealing with a ghostly enemy, powerlessness, and pain. It is in that sense that creating a permanent home for trust can operate in five key ways.

Cracking the firewall. When enemies share distorted and poisoned memories, neither of them really "knows" what the other one is talking about. Pain and anger are the essential ingredients any time an enemy is created. Even when we are in denial about them, enemies can drive people into isolation, leading such persons to become defensive and even to shut down altogether, convinced that "nobody can understand their pain." On one level, the request that we listen to someone else's pain can come across as a complaint because no one seems to understand the suffering (Benjamin 2017). Yet when people approach each other and take turns speaking from the heart and truly listening, the "enemy" can reach a very different and more constructive place.

Dissolving the fabricated enemy, the ghost, as I sometimes prefer to call this constructed entity, gets rid of the "anonymous" other, who otherwise appears simply as an evil warrior. When real people set off on the difficult "journey" to deconstruct or get rid of the enemy, the other turns into a full three-dimensional human being. Demonization is revealed for what it really is. "I have an enemy" and "I feel like an enemy" turn out to be one and the same thing. One's self-definition based on a rigidly held identity that all but rules any contact between "us" and "them" evaporates too.

Overcoming feelings of helplessness becomes possible. As long as we hold on to a misleading image of the enemy, we remain paralyzed, and we blow our differences with the other side out of proportion. But when we shed that image, the belief that "I can't do anything to help myself" gives way to very different questions, including "What can I do for you?" or "What can we do together?"

Converting pain into something better. No one is destined to live with oppressive and destructive pain. After one realizes that suffering is one of the cornerstones of any destructive relationship, both parties can learn how to deal with it together. We become able to transfer some of that pain to another person who is willing to listen and share our deepest emotions. At this point, the desire to protect each other begins to grow and brings a peace process with it. By contrast, if we deny pain, the isolation, which reinforces the image of the enemy, persists.

Moving beyond victimhood. We think of ourselves as victims. However, we are always more than just victims no matter how destructive a situation may have once seemed. In fact, the young people we host at Rondine are almost never themselves responsible for the pain that has been inflicted over the years, decades, or even centuries. Instead, if they are victims, it is because they remain obsessed with poisoned memories, which become fertile ground for polarization and radical action. Under this circumstance, the only option is to choose a path to move beyond victimhood and begin developing productive relationships with the other—a choice that might have seemed out of the question.

To coin one last term that might never find its way into everyday English, we can think of all of this as nurturing "two-way harmony," which is very different from the kinds of relationships we see in conflict settings today. Its definition in our hypothetical dictionary would run something like this:

> Two-way harmony describes the relationship between people who first decided to have a relationship that was based on believing that unconditional and respectful listening to the other and dealing with painful feelings that get left behind by intractable conflict can bring people together in the "interstitial time," or the time and space between people in which genuine human interaction can take place.

THE TIME TO COMMUNICATE

At the same time, we know that we have a lot to learn about how to do what we are already doing better. Even more importantly, we will continue to adapt the Rondine Method so it can become useful in other settings, something Charles Hauss will also try to do in his conclusion to this book.

We have already taken a few tentative steps in that direction. As I noted earlier we started the Fourth High School Year of Excellence in 2015, which provides a kind of domestic study abroad program for between twenty-five and thirty teenagers each year. The Italian Ministry of Education allowed students to spend their fourth (next to last) high school year in formally approved study abroad programs. Ours provides an international experience even though the students do not leave Italian soil. Instead, they spend a year living in nearby Arezzo and take the bus each morning a few kilometers so that they spend the school day studying with our international students at Rondine as part of what we call the Ulysses Path, which combines the Rondine Method with the curriculum normally taught in a conventional Italian high school (*liceo*).

World House graduates (whom we call *Rondini d'Oro*) have also taken the lead in spreading the Rondine Method beyond Italy's borders. They were largely responsible for the leadership project on global armaments spending, which got us to the United Nations in 2019 and set a chain of events in motion that ultimately led to this book. More importantly, another group of them introduced the project in Sierra Leone in which our graduates from several countries organized a larger group of young people to begin the reconciliation effort during the recent election campaign, which I discussed in chapter 1.

Like the two-year program, these initiatives and anything else we introduce in the future will not involve huge evolutionary leaps. Instead, they will remain true to the key concepts that are the heart of everything we do at Rondine. These initiatives will be anchored in four working hypotheses.

Improved Communication Skills to Build Trust

Our first working hypothesis should be familiar given what I've already written. The entire Rondine model is based on a worldview in which education and training can spark human renewal by combining a growing self-awareness that leads to better interpersonal relationships. This worldview links with the public sphere by stimulating community building, political action, and celebration. In other words, the relational space serves as a microcosm in which a Buber-like "I" and "thou" produce dialogues that lead toward an "us," which is inclusive and constantly expanding. Without it, relationships can collapse in the ways you have already seen not only in these pages but in the rest of our lives.

Beyond Rationality

That, in turn, leads us to implications we drew from Gregory Bateson's (2000) work, which marked one of the first times that an established scholar questioned the degree to which we systematically rely on rational approaches to solving our problems. Our attention must remain fixed on the ways people "translate" the words and thoughts of another into a common "world language." In particular, Bateson helped us see the damage that can be done when we explain what people do and think in ways that they never intended. Bateson and others demonstrated just how close the connection between the spoken and the unspoken can be. If, however, we find ways of meaningfully connecting their seemingly different signals and simplifying the connection between them, dialogue can become fruitful indeed. If not, a disagreement can lead to an ever-deteriorating relationship and its collapse, wiping out whatever trust that ever existed.

On Translation

We also have a lot to learn about how we can turn literal translation into true comprehension. This problem extends far beyond conflict resolution. As any analyst who has worked in multiple languages can attest, it is never easy to see what something means when you have to cross lines of difference, whether they be linguistic (in Todorov's case) or emotional (as at Rondine). He realized that he had to dig into the often-unspoken assumptions made when using any of the languages he wrote in. In our case, we must do exactly the same thing when we take part in a dialogue with the other.

The next path will have us spend more time exploring the psychosocial origins of any relationship. How can we create a resilient "relational space for trust"? It is true that we don't have an innate or built-in desire or aptitude for building that kind of relationship, which means that it will not automatically appear whenever we think we need it.

Medieval philosophers, for example, talked about "habitus," or the way similar people typically viewed the world. Today, we can think of it more in terms of the ways our worldviews are transmitted to us from birth onward, which prepare us for the kinds of relationships that we will embrace as adults.

Our work at Rondine is a contribution to this line of research. But we still have to explore the roots of the ways ongoing relationships unfold. What we have learned about caregiving takes us part of the way there. But fully understanding that connection and finding "cures" for all of its downsides will require research in any number of disciplines that will evolve our work and that of the experts we have drawn on over the years.

Finding the Time to Communicate

Rondine has always worked with other educational institutions from around the world with whom we have conducted training programs and have cooperated on peacebuilding and reconciliation initiatives. Some of them— including the Americans who have contributed to this book—have led us to think long and hard about the two-year commitment we ask our students to make. That makes our program unique but also makes it expensive and hard to reproduce by an organization that does not have our resources—let alone a village of its own!

We are convinced that the Rondine Method requires the amount of time and the physical distance that goes hand in hand with living in a community that is largely isolated from the chaos of the larger world. We have every intention of continuing the World House more or less as it is.

At the same time, we know that we will have to find other ways of creating something equivalent to the length of time students spend together. There must be other ways to replicate key parts of the Rondine experience in far less time and in far less idyllic settings. Our challenge will be to help people find other pathways toward making the choices and building the family-like and trauma-free relationships that we achieve in our residential program.

We need to consider these options because we reject the idea that societies are programmed to evolve in any one, preordained way. After all, no one chooses to be born at any given place at any given time or become part of any given social unit. Still, there are always other choices persons make, and those choices theoretically could be made in any setting.

So the real challenge is to figure out other and even faster ways of building the virtuous circles that expand mutual trust and constructive relationships in a wide variety of settings. A snapshot-like summary of what we've seen so far in this book should convince you that it can be done.

Every conflict can bring with it a heavy dose of pain and suffering if we fail to acknowledge and explore those emotions. We can get rid of the "poison" of traumatic events by helping individuals grow in ways that expand their relational space. We can create a community in which the "us," which is purely transactional, turns into a community because we have crossed a mental bridge that emphasizes sharing and creates more of a communal "us." To mix metaphors a bit, we find ourselves in the same boat together, and in time, we find ways of moving forward by adopting a common view of the world and its needs.

While the old American adage, "separate but equal," never made sense in the history of race relations, we might think instead of the phrase, "distinct but equal." Today's leading psychotherapists, like Jessica Benjamin, might argue that respect for different and distinct others is a precondition that opens a safe and shared space to foster authentic relationships.

Between Memory and Complex Thinking

All of this leads to a second conclusion about the Rondine Method, which could take us far beyond anything we have done so far. It forces us to confront one final existential paradox. How can we make sense of and expand what I've referred to as the stability of the relational space at a time when, as the cliché would have it, change is the only constant? As hard as it may be to believe, we now know how to build stable relationships that are different from those we have ever before experienced when dealing with intractable conflict. We can pick up on the very brief moments of discovery that happen at a place like Rondine and convert them into something that isn't fleeting but lasts indefinitely.

Here, it helps to draw on some of the insights associated with the French *Annales* school. As its generation of world-famous historians did, we ought to take a step back from concrete events and focus on the mindset or worldview through which people make sense of their surroundings. Just as was the case for those historians, our key lies in how we remember certain events and then weave them together into a kind of narrative. Oddly enough, doing so offers a monument to a past that can and does change over time because of our ongoing interpretations.

The Rondine Method can help everyone see two things. First, because our interpretations can and do change, those narratives or mental monuments can change in much the same way that images, mirages, and ghosts I've been talking about for the last four and a half chapters are changed at Rondine. Second, like the *Annales* historians, we have also learned that the whole is always much more than just the sum of its parts. The "whole" is always a function of the meaning we give it and how we react to the events taking place around us—especially how we react to what I've called relational shocks.

Because we can create relational spaces, what might seem like simply a dilemma about the way we communicate with each person turns into an existential crisis in which changes beyond our control and psychological dynamics that can be steered always leave us with room for maneuver. As both Benjamin and Bateson suggest, we can move from the dyadic connection between two people into a third side in which the two find ways to recognize and empathize with each other. In so doing, that mental addition turns both of those individuals into people who simultaneously give to and receive from each other.

If mutual recognition is to provide us with a degree of stability or consistency in a time of flux, we will need to share common memories and do so without eliminating the differences that will still exist among people who used to think of themselves as enemies. To do that, we have to engage in the kind of *complex thought* I first learned about from the French philosopher and sociologist Edgar Morin (1993, 2008), who introduced that term decades before American academics started writing about the science of complexity. Morin was also one of the first to think in terms of recursive and nonlinear processes in which two things can simultaneously cause each other. That has at least two implications for the Rondine Method. First, when taken to its limits, in both its French and American versions, complexity tells us that we cannot realistically hope to predict what emergent systems will look like. Still, we must do what we can to avoid the vicious cycles that make places like Rondine necessary in the first place while promoting the virtuous ones that Rondine works to create.

We are drawn to Morin in concluding, too, because he always advises us to proceed confidently—he was still doing so at age 100 when I wrote these words. Although he was never personally interested in the kind of suffering and trauma that we deal with at Rondine, he understood that truly recognizing the other requires the same kind of break with deterministic rationality. This is the break we foster at Rondine. Unlike what behavioral psychologists and most other social scientists tell us, we can't (re)create what I call the relational space unless we think in terms of recursive systems and dig more deeply into the parts of the mind that traditional science tends to ignore. It is only by exploring these new philosophical and empirical pathways that we can transcend the immediate; escape from the mundane events that seem to entrap us; and overcome the addictions, weakness, and uncertainties that plague our world today.

> Many people—many nations—can find themselves believing, more or less consciously, that "every stranger is an enemy." For the most part, this conviction lies buried in the mind like some latent infection.

So wrote Primo Levi in the introduction to *If This Is a Man*, in which he wrote about his memories of the way that fears can not only take over our own minds but also feed the fears of others too.

Part 2

RESPONSES TO THE RONDINE METHOD

Rondine Cittadella Della Pace

AN OPEN-AIR LABORATORY ABOUT INTERGROUP CONFLICT AND INTERGROUP CONTACT THEORY

Ariela Pagani, Anna Bertoni, A. Garuglieri, and Raffaella Iafrate

This chapter offers a psychosocial perspective on the work done at Rondine Cittadella della Pace and provides the theoretical background for the evaluation research conducted by the Family Studies and Research University Centre of the Università Cattolica del Sacro Cuore of Milan (Italy).

A Reading of the Experience through the Eyes of Social Psychology

Rondine Cittadella della Pace is a sort of "open-air laboratory of social psychology" in which it is possible to see the main psychosocial theories related to intergroup conflict and the possible strategies for overcoming it (Iafrate and Bertoni 2019). Research conducted in this field since the mid-1950s has shown that the clearest manifestation of the presence of conflict between different groups is witnessed by the presence of attitudes, emotions, and behaviors of members of two groups: a group that tends to express a form of favoritism toward the group one belongs to (*in-group*) and the other, identified as "rival" or "other," that tends to express a form of discrimination against the in-group (*out-group*). The pro in-group favoritism and the discrimination against the out-group can be found in the "theory of social identity" (Tajfel and Turner 1979), which affirms the intrinsic and original social dimension of the self as the most convincing explanation. The theory of social identity shows that when people express a favoritism toward the in-group and a discrimination against the out-group, they are just trying to defend themselves and their identity. Therefore, we could state that we are faced with a kind of human "survival mechanism." In this sense, conflict is part of human nature. The dimension of social identity, in fact, leads people to aspire to a positive social identity, and such positivity is linked to the fact that everyone will embrace their own group (in-group) as much as possible compared to an "other" group (out-group). The in-group acquires value when the out-group is devalued at the same time.

We could say that the experience of Rondine turns the lessons of social psychology into a tangible, concrete reality. Those who experience Rondine, in fact, often face a conflict of loyalty. In other words, it is as if, regarding their companions, each of the participants asked themselves "How can I reconcile the fact that I like you because I know you and you have these characteristics that meet my personal needs but you are also part of a country that is at war with mine (me as a part of my country)? How can I, who carry both these dimensions of identity within myself, cope with this internal conflict?" This dialectic between the "I" and the "we," which is inside the identity of each person, is not always peacefully harmonious within the self; on the contrary, it is always potentially conflictual. For this reason, one of Rondine's objective is not to eliminate conflict but to become aware that it is an integral part of the human being and that it is necessary to learn how to manage it while also recognizing its creative and constructive potentialities and not be dominated by its destructive side. So what are the variables that can limit the impact of these mechanisms of discrimination and favoritism, which, at times, can exacerbate the conflict by leading to a narcissistic and partisan favoritism of the in-group and a discrimination of the out-group in deadly terms? And what are the factors that can moderate these natural and human tendencies? These are the key questions that guide the recent perspectives that analysts of the social psychology of groups are asking, and these are also the questions that drive a substantial part of the challenge of Rondine's project.

Alongside the research on the identification of influential factors on intergroup conflict, another line of research is designed to elaborate specific strategies for overcoming conflict. Among the scholars who first dealt with this aspect, Allport (1954) with his "intergroup contact theory" theorized the factors that allow a change of attitudes and behaviors between two conflicting groups, affirming that the decrease in intergroup tensions and hostility is due to contact between the individuals who belong to them. In his view, prejudice and discrimination arise from a lack of knowledge among members of different groups. Therefore, if people are offered the opportunity to meet individuals belonging to the out-group, they will find that basically many prejudices and stereotypes are wrong. According to Allport (1954; see also Pettigrew 1998), mere contact between groups is not sufficient to improve intergroup relations. Rather, to reduce bias, the contact situation must meet the following conditions:

- The contact must take place between people of equal status.
- The contact must be prolonged.

- The contact must take place in a context of institutional support (i.e., in a context supported by social norms conducive to contact between groups).
- There must be a superordinate or common goal for both groups to support.

Only under these conditions can the contact lead to the reduction of prejudice and conflict.

From the 1980s onward, intergroup contact theory has been deepened and expanded, highlighting the conditions that can favor the expansion of the positive effects of contact. In particular, two main models have emerged. The model by Brewer and Miller (1984) supports the need to place less emphasis on social categories to "personalize" the situation. The model by Hewstone and Brown (1986) emphasizes the importance of maintaining both categories of social belonging and personal characteristics, recognizing "dual identities," or rather, recognizing the complex identity structure of the person, which has both individual and relational dimensions.

If the experience at Rondine Cittadella della Pace begins with the process of decategorization/recategorization, which allows us to see the person behind the enemy (according to the model developed by Brewer and Miller), its greatest success is reached when, in addition to recognition of the other "beyond" their belonging, it allows the recognition of the other "with" their belonging. In other words, according to the model by Hewstone and Brown, when the encounter with the "enemy" becomes the encounter with a person to whom I recognize a common humanity, but at the same time their diversity, I recognize them as people who keep their identity exactly as I keep my own. Recognizing the commonality in the other, but also their differences, is the fundamental passage that the challenge of Rondine poses among its goals.

Toward the Evaluation Research

As researchers, we have been asked to prove, evaluate, and measure whether, indeed, Rondine's ambitious and visionary challenge concretely made the difference for those students who were lucky enough to meet this reality by participating in the training project.

Why should we evaluate a project that has already drawn so much praise over the years, including a nomination for the Nobel Peace Prize? Because a formative experience can be very satisfying, exciting, and intriguing but not necessarily make a significant change in people's lives. Starting from these premises, the interest was born of conducting research whose general purpose was to observe and evaluate the Rondine Method as the current context of application of intergroup contact theory and, more generally, observe how the theories that we have just described are used concretely and specifically in that environment. Therefore, we conducted evaluation research on the Rondine Method. However, before going into our results, it is important to underline what we mean by evaluation research to remove any ambiguity from the term *evaluation*. In fact, we know that the word is often associated with feelings of judgment, which can make people feel "under investigation," put under a microscope, and even a little threatened.

Evaluation research, however, does not evaluate to judge, or to find a "right" and a "wrong," but rather, to "measure" and give "value." Evaluation research tries to measure because it leads to questioning the extent of change produced by an intervention. Evaluation research also evaluates in the sense of giving value to the object that is being evaluated. In fact, it investigates aspects of the experience looking for the whole space for change produced by it, knowing that this change is often generative. The design of an intervention assumes that things will change, but it may also happen that more change occurs than was originally planned or in ways that were not foreseen but that the evaluation research manages to identify and highlight. It is simply an external, trained gaze that often allows us to grasp not only the expected but even the unexpected and seeks to give meaning and value to an intervention in order to have an even greater impact later on.

But, again, what does it mean to evaluate? An assessment involves the systematic collection of information about the activities, characteristics, and results of programs and interventions aimed at people interested in judging how specific aspects of those programs and interventions have operated and affected the system. Evaluation research is, in fact, a kind of scientific research that requires a rigorous method of data collection in which all the steps must be explained so that they can be recognized and understood. Systematic rigor in data collection is essential within the scientific world in which every epistemic, theoretical, and methodological choice must be made explicit and shared so that each individual step can be traced back to the broader research framework and, if necessary, replicated, validated, or refuted.

When do we evaluate an intervention? Always, we could say. It is not only evaluated at the end. An intervention is evaluated before and during its implementation and at its end so that each of the steps can be connected to its outcomes. If an evaluation of an intervention is carried out, the evaluation is not separate from the intervention, but rather, it is built in to the practice and is integral to all of its phases.

What tools do we evaluate with? In order to understand a complex reality like the one that deals with people, relationships, and groups, we must apply a multimethodological approach (Wilkinson 1987) where different types of instruments can be used. In fact, many different points of view are needed to understand a complex reality, like looking at the same landscape from different heights of a mountain: there will be different perspectives, all partial but all capturing a true aspect of the landscape. By combining instruments of a different nature, we can not only have more indicators of the same reality (as in a movie set when you have multiple cameras to film the same scene) but also have qualitatively different points of view, each of them capturing a unique and specific appearance of the reality.

Who can benefit from evaluation research? It can be useful to those who took part in the intervention in different ways. It can be useful primarily to those who wanted the intervention and supported it because the evaluation documents the outcomes that emerged given the available funding. This kind of research can also be useful to those who conducted the intervention because, in a perspective of constant improvement, it is useful to know which actions have produced the most change. Finally, evaluation research can also be useful for those who took part in the intervention because the evaluation can be configured as an external examination of the project that highlights the changes and new directions that were tried. Those taking part in an intervention are interested in learning more about what happened.

Finding out what works can help orient and understand where you are. For example, learning about the results of an evaluation can be an important moment of growth and empowerment, which can even mark a "before" and an "after" phase in the larger project of those who receive an evaluation report. The evaluation research also can inform people who could participate in future interventions because it is useful to know what worked for those who have already been involved.

In other words, assessment makes it possible to be aware of the limits and potentials of the actions carried out, to make informed decisions, and to make sense of the work. It lets everyone know whether the intervention makes sense and produces change. Finally, it makes the results public and thereby increases knowledge (Leone and Prezza 1999).

Evaluation research can also be designed not only to measure and manage what happened but also to act as a real guide to social action. This is the classic action research (Lewin 1946), which provides, on the one hand, an analysis of subjects and, on the other hand, improves what the subjects themselves do because they can not only share and benefit from the results of the research but also, through the results, reach a greater level of understanding and a deeper awareness of the existing reality, which can often produce a quantum leap in the subjects' effectiveness.

In our case, the first constructive outcome emerged during the pilot phase, which is for the researchers a fundamental moment of the research cycle because it allows the development of the goals, the operationalization of the topics of interest (e.g., How is the conflict measured?), the definition of constructs, and the identification of objectives. In the pilot phase, we were guided not only by a close analysis of the psychosocial literature but also by a deep and questioning listening to the Rondini d'Oro (Rondine alumni) who entrusted their stories to us. It was not difficult to grasp that these stories were filled with themes that reappeared in all the narratives, especially the transcendent theme—identity. Therefore, it seems that the work of Rondine does not "only" have implications for the deconstruction of the image of the enemy but also has very important implications for one's identity and being seen as belonging, both of which seem to go through a process of deconstruction and reconstruction. When talking about their first days at Rondine Cittadella della Pace, the students of the World House described themselves through their collective, or social, identity: "'I am Armenian,' he said, challenging me" or "'I am Azerbaijani,' I said, emphasizing every word." In these stories, the collective part (i.e., group membership) occupies a lot of space, and the description of themselves in terms of personal identity is all but missing.

These findings lead to two reflections. The first one is suggested by clinical psychologists. The parallel between the way in which the students of the World House describe themselves (I cannot describe myself but only to whom I belong) is anything but random. It is common for those who have been distorted and involved in painful experiences to feel overwhelmed. *Being overwhelmed* is a term often associated with traumatic experiences, and it means that your personal identity is totally submerged in deeply rooted pain. So if I am overwhelmed by pain, I cannot or I will not see myself. The second reflection is suggested by the experts in social psychology. Defining oneself as only belonging to a group that is an enemy of another group suggests how identity often has its roots in conflict. We could say, "We have an enemy, so we are. But the question is, if we no longer have an enemy, who are we?" and again, "Is it possible to give birth to a 'personal self' within this group identity?"

At the end of their stay at Rondine Cittadella della Pace, the students describe themselves using statements that tell us more about their own personal identity: "Who am I? I am a Rondine." These descriptions tell us of the possibility that they are better able to "see themselves" and "recognize themselves" in a historical context by the end of their stay at Rondine Cittadella della Pace. This is what Rondine is capable of fostering and what the evaluation research helps us capture. It was interesting to note that the reflections made on personal identity also emerge in relation to the students' perceived identity of the enemy. Early on, they perceived the enemy not as a single person but as "those who have tried to extinguish you" (i.e., a generic and disembodied people), while at the end of the experience, the enemy assumes a face. "The enemies today have a name; these faces have become people first and then with great effort, friends." In conclusion, to work on the conflict, one has to work on identity on a personal, a group, a social, and a collective level. Only through this work on the deepest aspects of the self can we grasp creative spaces of hope, which can inhabit the future of the "children of war" so that they finally become "whole people." The Rondini d'Oro have become people who have reacquired their own identity.

The Research

The evaluation research conducted by the Family Studies and Research University Centre of the Università Cattolica del Sacro Cuore of Milan (Italy) aims to answer the following questions (Pagani and Garuglieri 2019):

- Is there a change in the way participants in the Rondine experiment perceive themselves and their in-group?
- Is there a change in the way participants perceive the enemy and the out-group?

In particular, in this chapter, we will present the results about the following:

- How the perception of closeness between oneself and one's own in-group, between oneself and one's own out-group, and between one's in-group and one's out-group changes over time.
- How the perception of the in-group's and out-group's humanity or dehumanization changes over time.

METHOD

Procedure

The research began in January 2017 and produced its first results in June 2018. It was divided into three waves: beginning of the academic year (T1, October 2017), at the middle of the academic year (T2, February 2018), and end of the academic year (T3, May 2018). The months between January and September 2017 were useful for preparing the research instruments and conducting the pilot study described above in order to get suggestions for making changes to the preexisting materials and to building new ones from scratch (figure 6.1).

Participants

The World House sample included thirteen people.[1] Of these, eleven were present in the first wave; ten, in the second; and nine, in the third. Eight were women, and five were men. Participants were between twenty-two and thirty-one years of age (M = 25.09; DS = 2.62). Seven were from the Caucasus and

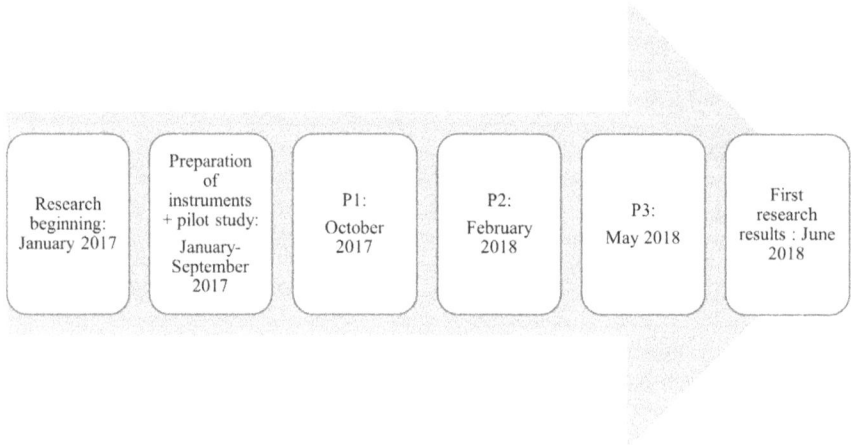

Figure 6.1. Research Phases

Eastern Europe (e.g., Armenia, Azerbaijan, Georgia, Kosovo, and Serbia), four were from countries in the Middle East (e.g., Lebanon and Palestine), and four were from Mali. The participants have diversified academic backgrounds, but all have at least their undergraduate degrees. Of the students, 63.6 percent are Christian, 9.1 percent are Muslim, and the rest declared that they belong to another religion not included in the questionnaire.[2] Finally, 18.2 percent do not belong to any religion. Among the Christians, 45.5 percent are Catholic, 9.1 percent are Apostolic, and 9.1 percent are Orthodox. Among those who belong to a religion, 27.3 percent consider themselves very observant; 18.2 percent, fairly observant; 27.3 percent, not very observant; and 27.3 percent, not observant at all. Almost all of the participants (90.9 percent) report that their family is very much in agreement with their participation in Rondine Cittadella della Pace; 50.4 percent, that the family has greatly supported them; and 45.5 percent, that the family has supported them enough. Almost half of the students (45.6 percent) have a family member who has been directly involved in the conflict. The examples that the students mentioned included, for example, the wounding of a brother, a father in the military, fighting in their hometowns, or the forced emigration of the parents during the conflict.

Measures

For data collection, the researchers decided to adopt a multimethodological approach (Wilkinson 1987). Specifically, three different instruments were used, two of which were qualitative and one, quantitative: focus group, heraldic shield, and self-administered questionnaire. In all phases of the research, the focus group was the first instrument that was proposed to the participants; subsequently, two heraldic shields were compiled (one on the in-group and one on the out-group), and finally, the self-administered questionnaire was given. Participants were asked to read and sign informed consent to data collection, explaining to them that this would mean authorizing the analysis of their answers for research purposes while maintaining anonymity.

Focus Group

The focus group is a data collection technique for social research based on the discussion between a small group of people, invited by one or more moderators to talk to each other, in depth, of the topic being investigated (Corrao 2000). As part of this research, in all three waves, a researcher asked the students of the World House the following questions:

- What does the word *conflict* mean to you?
- Where, in your opinion, is the conflict in human life?
- In your opinion, what can be done to resolve a conflict?
- What does the word *peace* mean to you?

Participants were asked to give their consent to recording their responses. The students of the World House were allowed to express themselves in English and/or French if it was difficult for them to find the right words in Italian (remember that the first focus group was proposed to the students of the World House three months after their arrival to Rondine). The focus group lasted about an hour.

Heraldic Shield

The heraldic shield, inspired by the heraldic coats of arms, is an instrument adapted by Fulmer (1983), which is widely used in both training and research environments. In the case of this research, two versions (figures 6.2 and 6.3) were used with the aim of bringing out the representation that each subject has of their own group (in-group) and of their own enemy group (out-group) through the request to draw (and then explain briefly in words) the following:

- The most positive side of the in-group/out-group
- The most negative side of the in-group/out-group
- The biggest hope for the in-group/out-group

Before proceeding with the drawing and the brief explanation, the participants were asked to identify and write on each of the two heraldic shields to which group they belonged and to which enemy group they would refer to. The subjects drew their heraldic shields individually. In each wave, participants had approximately forty minutes to complete this instrument in both versions.

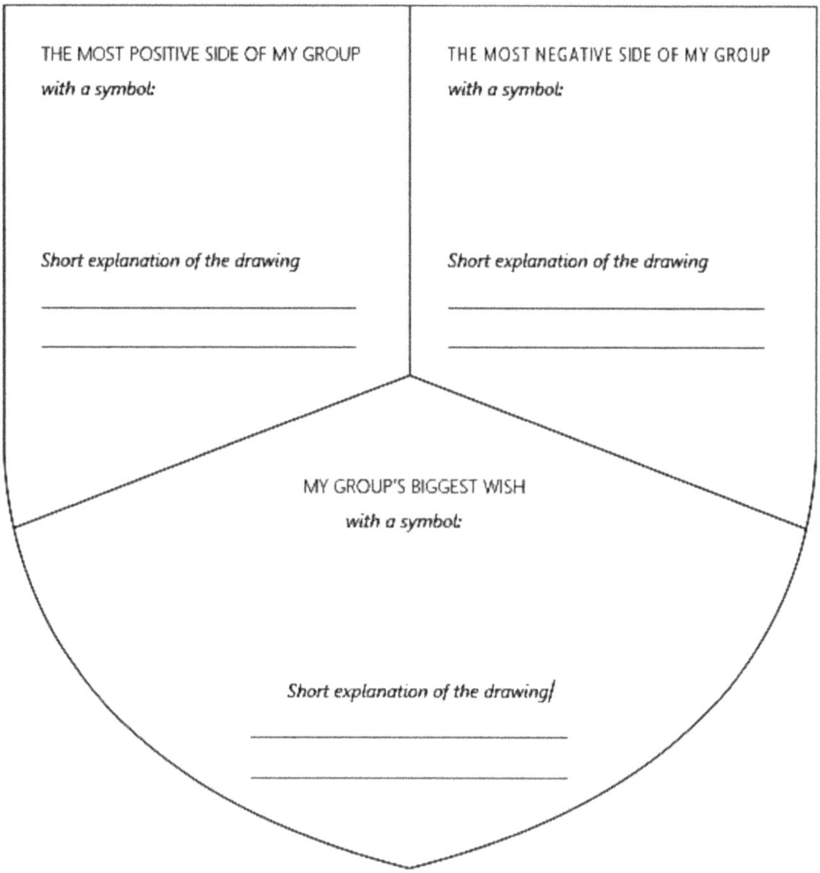

Figure 6.2.   Heraldic Shield Referring to the In-group

Self-Administered Questionnaire

The last instrument used is a self-administered questionnaire, which, in addition to questions related to the sociodemographic characteristics of the participants, included different scales: Sense of Coherence Scale (SOC; Antonovsky 1987), Generativity Scale (McAdams and De St. Aubin 1992),[3] Adult Consumer Empowerment Scale (ACES; Rogers, Chamberlin, Ellison, and Crean 1997), Conflict Communication Scale (Goldstein 1999), Inclusion of Other in the Self Scale (IOS; Aron, Aron, and Smollan 1992), dehumanization scale (Capozza, Trifiletti, Vezzali, and Favara 2013), Ethno-Cultural Identity Conflict Scale (EICS; Ward, Stuart, and Kus 2011), Ethos of Conflict Scale (Bar-Tal, Sharvit, Halperin, and Zafran 2012), Rye Forgiveness Scale (RFS; Rye et al. 2001), and semantic differential (ad hoc).

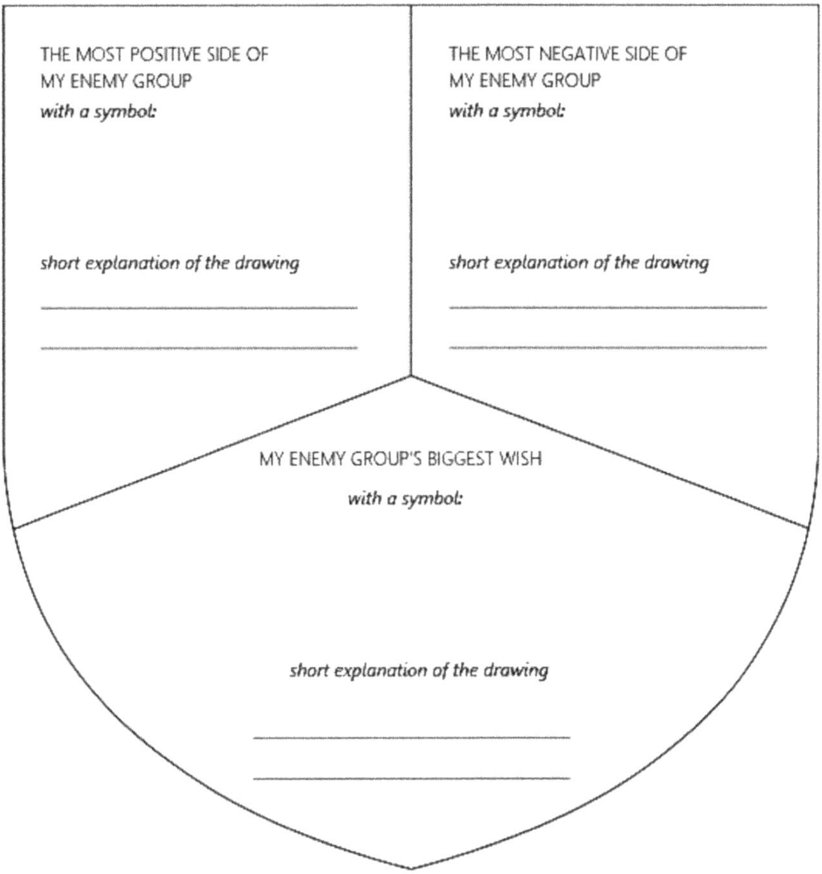

THE MOST POSITIVE SIDE OF
MY ENEMY GROUP
with a symbol:

short explanation of the drawing
_____

_____

THE MOST NEGATIVE SIDE OF
MY ENEMY GROUP
with a symbol:

short explanation of the drawing
_____

_____

MY ENEMY GROUP'S BIGGEST WISH

with a symbol:

short explanation of the drawing
_____

_____

Figure 6.3. Heraldic Shield Referring to the Out-group

In addition to specific measures on the conflict and on the perception of one's own in-group (or one's own identity) and one's own out-group (that is the identity of the enemy), some measures were included in the questionnaire to evaluate other ways the students could have changed as a result of the experience at Rondine Cittadella della Pace. In each wave, participants had approximately sixty minutes to complete this instrument. The students of the World House were also given a copy of the questionnaire in English to make it easier for them to understand the questions. Here, we will limit ourselves only to those scales we used in the evaluative part of our research.

A) *Inclusion of Other in the Self Scale* (IOS; Aron et al. 1992). The IOS scale consists of a series of six Venn diagrams, each showing two circles in various overlapping stages, from circles not overlapping at all (1) to

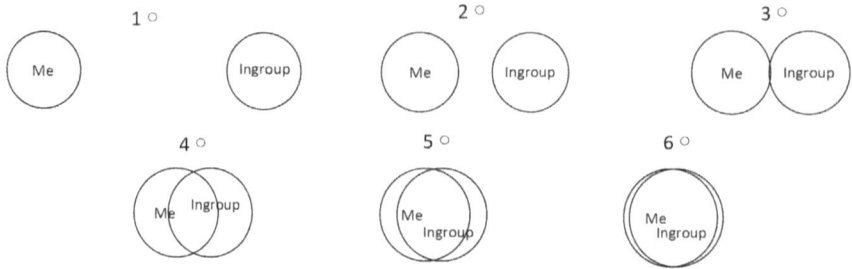

Figure 6.4.   Inclusion of Other in the Self Scale. Relationship between Self and One's Own In-group.

circles almost completely overlapping (6). The circles are drawn in such a way that the area of each circle is equal and constant and the degree of overlap, created on the six steps, is progressive. In this research, three different IOS scales were used, asking subjects to choose the set of circles that best represents the following:

• The relationship between oneself and one's own in-group (figure 6.4)
• The relationship between oneself and one's own out-group (figure 6.5)
• The relationship between one's own in-group and one's own out-group (figure 6.6)

Values close to or equal to 1 indicate that the parts are perceived far from each other, while values close to or equal to 6 indicate that the parts are perceived as close together.

Dehumanization scale (Capozza et al. 2013). This scale assesses dehumanization (i.e., perceiving a person or group as lacking human features) through four unique human traits (i.e., reasoning, rationality, morality, and understanding) and four nonuniquely human traits (i.e., instinct, drive, impulsiveness, and impetus). Participants first rated the in-group and then the out-group on both

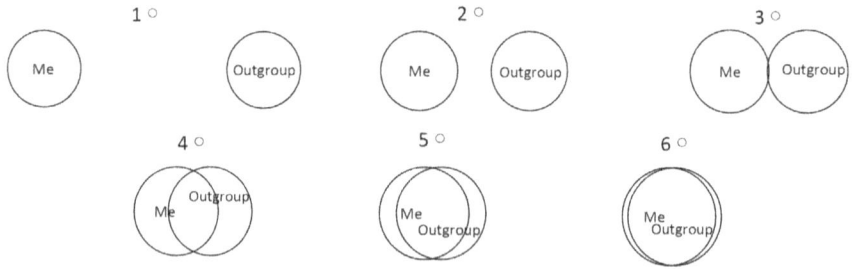

Figure 6.5.   Inclusion of Other in the Self Scale. Relationship between Self- and One's Own Out-group.

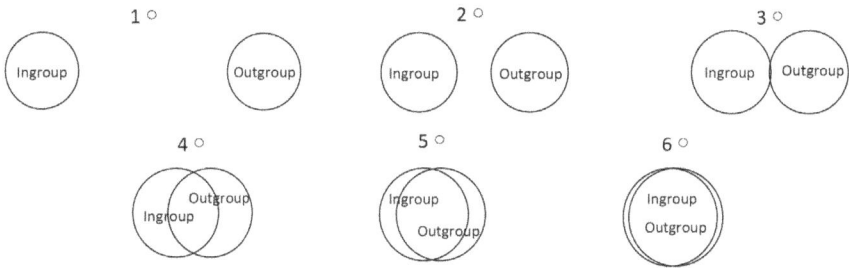

Figure 6.6. Inclusion of Other in the Self Scale. Relationship between One's Own in-group and One's Own out-group.

kinds of traits, responding on a 7-point Likert scale (from 1 = *absolutely false* to 7 = *absolutely true*).

RESULTS

In this section only the results related to the two scales described above and based on the comparison between the first and the last waves will be presented. These results allow us to observe the changes at the end of the first year among students of the World House at Rondine Cittadella della Pace.

Perception of Closeness

In general, these analyses showed that for the students of the World House there was a perception of greater closeness between themselves and their own in-group compared to the experience between themselves and their own out-group or between their own in-group and their own out-group (figure 6.7). Specifically,

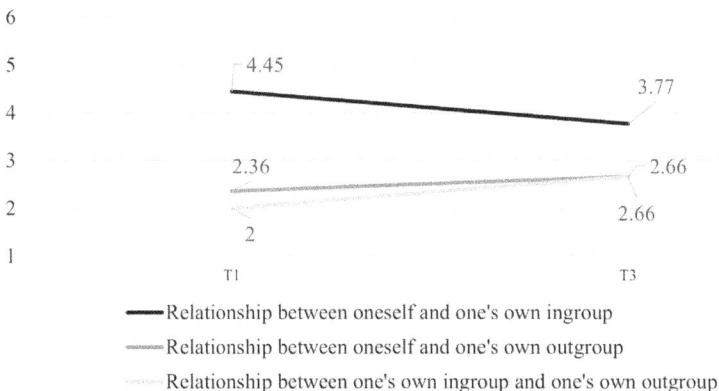

Figure 6.7. Perception of Closeness

descriptive analyses revealed that the perception of closeness between oneself and one's own in-group decreased between T1 and T3 (T1: M = 4.45; DS = 1.29; P3: M = 3.77; DS = 1.56). Paired sample nonparametric t-tests, performed by comparing the waves, were nonetheless all nonstatistically significant (T1–T3: p = 0.33); that is, there were no statistically significant changes in the levels of perception of closeness between oneself and one's own in-group during the waves. Regarding the perception of closeness between self and one's own out-group, descriptive analyses showed how this perception increased between T1 and T3 (T1: M = 2.36; DS = 1.20; T3: M = 2.66; DS = 1.11), but the paired-sample nonparametric t-test did not show statistically significant changes in the levels of perception of closeness between oneself and one's own out-group during the waves (T1–T3: p = 0.25). Finally, regarding the perception of closeness between one's own in-group and one's own out-group, although the paired-sample nonparametric t-test was not significant (T1–T3: p = 0.19), descriptive analyses showed how this perception gradually increased over time (P1: M = 2.00; DS = 1.18; T3: M = 2.66; DS = 1.93).

Dehumanization

As for the uniquely human traits referring to one's own in-group, descriptive analyses showed that the perception of one's own in-group as human decreased between P1 and P3 (M = 5.27, DS = 0.91; T3: M = 5.05, DS = 0.84), although the paired-sample nonparametric t-test was not significant (T1–T3: p = 0.83). As for the nonuniquely human traits, the paired-sample nonparametric t-test was not statistically significant (T1–T3: p = 0.17), but descriptive analyses showed that the perception of one's own in-group as less human increased during the waves (M = 4.38, DS = 1.53; T3: M = 5.07, DS = 0.78). This means that one's own in-group is perceived as dehumanizing over time (figure 6.8).

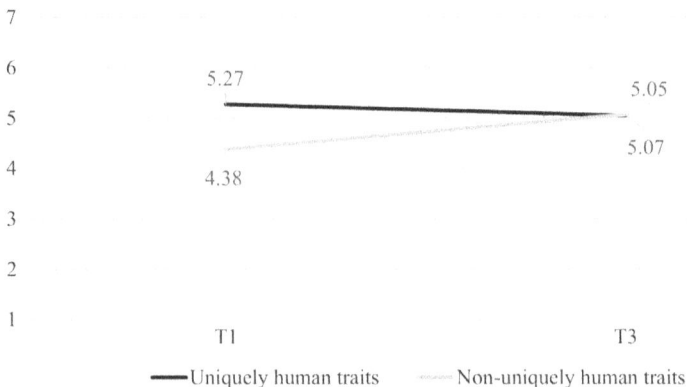

Figure 6.8. Perception of Humanity/Dehumanization: In-group

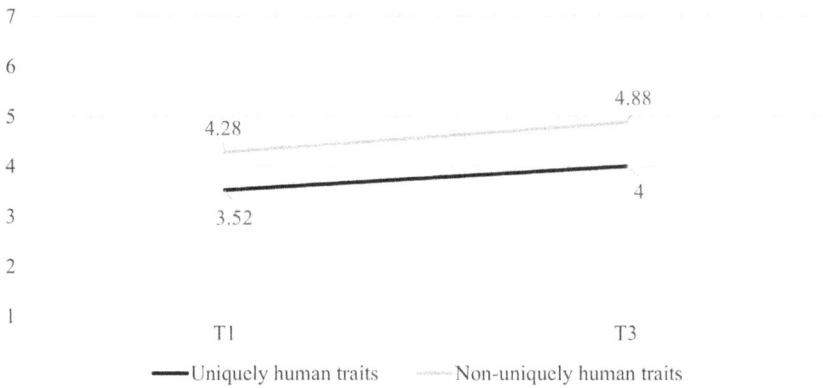

Figure 6.9.   Perception of Humanity/Dehumanization: Out-group

As for the uniquely human traits referring to one's own out-group, descriptive analyses showed that the perception of one's own out-group as human increased between T1 and T3 ($M = 3.52$, $DS = 1.11$; T3: $M = 4.00$, $DS = 0.95$), although the paired-sample nonparametric t-test was not significant (T1–T3: $p = 0.12$). As for the nonuniquely human traits, the paired-sample nonparametric t-tests were not statistically significant (T1–T3: $p = 0.49$), but descriptive analyses showed that the perception of one's own out-group as less human increased during the waves (T1: $M = 4.28$, $DS = 1.54$; T3: $M = 4.88$, $DS = .55$; figure 6.9). This means that one's own out-group is perceived, at the same time, as more human and more dehumanizing, although the mean values of the dehumanization (nonuniquely human traits) are greater than the mean values of the humanization (uniquely human traits).

Nevertheless, if we compare the mean scores of dehumanization (nonuniquely human traits) of the in-group and the out-group, the descriptive analyses showed that the in-group is perceived as more dehumanizing than the out-group over time (figure 6.10).

Conclusions

The evaluation research presented in this chapter was designed to explore the intergroup conflict, analyzing the level of pro-group favoritism and out-group discrimination among the students of the World House and analyze their changes over time from October 2017 to June 2018.

Thanks to the self-administered questionnaire, it was possible to understand and describe the change of the students of the World House in relation to some more specific constructs, which can be found in the "in-group versus

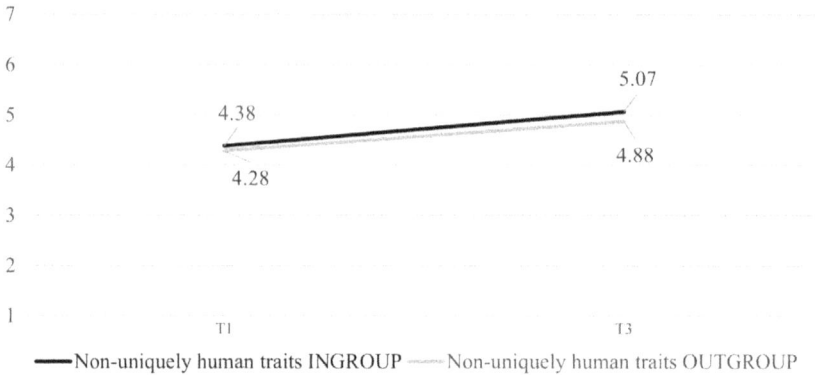

Figure 6.10. Perception of In-group and Outgroup's Non-Uniquely Human Traits (Dehumanization)

out-group" literature. Specifically, descriptive analyses and paired-sample nonparametric *t*-tests conducted on the questionnaire data have shown that the participants tend to favor the in-group and discriminate against the out-group. There is a greater perception of closeness between oneself and one's own in-group than between oneself and one's own out-group and between one's own in-group and one's own out-group. Nonetheless, this general result needs further research. It is possible to observe how the perception of closeness between oneself and one's own in-group decreased over time and how the perception of closeness between oneself and one's own out-group and between one's own in-group and one's own out-group, on the contrary, increased. Students at the World House do not question their identity (the closeness between oneself and one's own in-group does not change in a statistically significant way), but they manage to perceive their own in-group and their own out-group in a less distant and antagonistic way.

Referring to humanity/dehumanization, the results showed that both uniquely human traits and nonuniquely human traits belong to both the in-group and the out-group. In other words, the results deriving from the dehumanization scale show that "I am not better than the other." My enemy and I are linked because we share in particular nonhuman traits, that is, aspects of fragility and limitations.

Research is still in progress, but these first results appear to be promising. We hope to be able to confirm and deepen them at the end of the two-year period that the students spend at the World House at Rondine Cittadella della Pace.

Notes

1. There are normally two subgroups of roughly the same size at Rondine, which means that there are usually about thirty students at the World House. The first subgroup, present from the previous year, carries on its second year, while the second subgroup arrives to begin its first year. In this way, the World House always comprises *senior* and *junior* students. In 2016, Rondine chose not to have new students arrive so that it could conduct an internal reorganization. This is why the year 2017–2018 was characterized by the absence of a senior group. Because of this, the sample object of the research is composed of half of the typical number of international students, which is thirteen subjects.

2. Options to the question related to religious affiliation: Christian (specify which confession), Hebrew, Muslim, Hindu, Buddhist, other religion (specify), no religious affiliation.

3. The theme of generativity is at the heart of the relational-symbolic approach, to which the work of the Family Studies and Research University Centre is dedicated. See, in particular, Family Studies and Research University Centre (2018) and Bertoni, Parise, and Iafrate (2012).

CHAPTER 7

The Rondine Method and Foreign Policy

Michael David Kaiser

One of the first things students learn in foreign policy is the 3Ds, not three-dimensional thinking but (1) diplomacy, (2) development, and (3) defense.

The 3Ds are fundamental for understanding foreign policy. Through *diplomacy* we learn to build trust and friendships. We also form alliances of mutual respect. Diplomacy is the least expensive of the 3Ds but the most cost effective. Next is *development*. By investing financial and human resources in countries, we can reduce poverty, promote public health, enhance education, create jobs, stimulate local economies, improve human rights, and reduce the likelihood of government instability and violent extremism. Finally, *defense* is the third and most expensive of the 3Ds. Ideally, if the first and second Ds are done correctly, the third D is not necessary. In fact, defense represents a failure of the first two Ds and is more likely to produce mistrust, rather than trust and long-term friendships.

Unfortunately, defense spending is on the rise in many countries even as funding for development and diplomacy is on the decline. What we would expect to be the last resort has instead become the first, and why we need the Rondine Method.

The Role for the Rondine Method in the 3Ds

A role for the Rondine Method in diplomacy is clear, but it should not end there. The Rondine Method is just as important in development and defense and goes beyond simply building diplomatic friendships and relationships with individuals. The Rondine Method can be applied to development policies and programs that people create, which, like the people themselves, are often conflicted. Think of the Rondine Method as a way of resolving conflict not just in people but also in the policies and programs that divide people.

To understand how the Rondine Method should be applied beyond diplomacy to include development, think about how development has traditionally been done. For more than a century, development has been Colonial in nature. What is needed is true Foreign Aid Reform that allows for locally led, rather than internationally led, interventions—interventions that operate from the *bottom up*, instead of the *top down*, and from the *inside out*, instead of the *outside in*.[1] Locally led interventions cost less, respond quicker, and are far more effective and more sustainable than interventions led from Geneva, New York, or Washington. These locally led interventions can be managed by faith-based groups, colleges and universities, and NGOs in-country rather than by international aid organizations abroad. Independence and self-determination can be established, instead of dependence on foreign assistance. What's more, these locally led interventions build better government relations for donor countries because more money gets into the affected countries, rather than into the pockets of private contractors and large, bureaucratic aid organizations. In effect, countries can solve their own problems, rather than expecting the international community to solve their problems for them. Finally, working locally also develops better intelligence in these countries, which is a growing concern as more and more countries become politically unstable and susceptible to homegrown terrorism.

The Benefits of Bottom-Up Thinking

No one knows local problems better than those who live in the local community. Whether it's birth defects, malnutrition, extreme poverty, corrupt government, or environmental disasters, people locally know their problems best. What local residents *do not* need is someone telling them what's wrong or what to do; rather, they need someone who will listen to them and take the time to develop an intervention *with* them, not *for* them. Donor nations and international aid organizations must also pursue interventions that are in a country's best interests, not in the best interests of donor countries and international aid organizations.

The Rondine Method can find a common language that makes people equal in diplomacy, as well as in development and defense. For development, Rondine can make interventions more effective by acting one country, one community, and one person at a time. Development efforts should not simply take an intervention off the shelf from one country and apply it to another. Every country is unique, and every community is unique, just as every person is unique. The Rondine Method knows this.

The Haiti Example

There is perhaps no better example of failed international diplomacy and development than in Haiti after the 2010 earthquake. Before the earthquake, it was almost impossible to get international aid groups to work in remote parts of Haiti. It was *too problematic*. Yet after the earthquake, international aid groups poured into the country because money was available. Unfortunately, these international aid organizations chose to deliver their interventions, not giving the Haitian people or the Haitian government what they wanted but instead, what the international aid organizations wanted to give them. Ten years later, Haiti is worse off today than it was before the earthquake, with literally billions of dollars spent on failed diplomacy and development (Keith 2021). It was widely reported that nearly one out of every two Americans gave money in support of Haiti's earthquake victims but that less than half of that money ever arrived in Haiti (Adelmann 2012). The Red Cross received half a billion dollars and built only six houses, instead using the money to pay down its own debts (Elliott and Sullivan 2015). Haitians received less than 1 percent of the money given by the United States. Ninety-nine percent went to the U.S. Department of Defense, the U.S. State Department, nongovernmental organizations (NGOs), and U.S. Agency for International Development (USAID) contractors (Wallace and Preston 2011). Clearly, diplomacy and development efforts in Haiti failed, benefiting the international community more than the Haitian people (Webster 2012).

What we learned from the Haitian earthquake is that international diplomacy and development must be reformed. The Rondine Method can play an important role in this reformation and improve development just as it has improved diplomacy. And if the Rondine Method can improve development and diplomacy, why not defense?

The Third D

The Rondine Method can make wars less likely and less severe. After wars in Vietnam, Iraq, and Afghanistan, the U.S. Department of Defense realized that the way forward was not to see entire countries as enemies but rather, to find allies within countries and build friendships and alliances (e.g., the Kurds in Syria). Indeed, defense leaders learned the way to peace was not through *shock and awe* to escalate violence but rather, through shared understanding to escalate trust and friendships; otherwise, wars can go on forever.

Developing Rondine interventions for defense may be more difficult than developing Rondine interventions for development and diplomacy; nonetheless, the same method applies: approach your enemy as your equal—with respect—and learn from one another to achieve a lasting, sustainable peace.

The Philippines Example

In the mid-1990s, USAID and Emory University were developing nutrition interventions in the Philippines to bring iron, iodine, folic acid, and vitamin A coverage to Southern Mindanao. On one trip, Abu Sayyaf guerillas beheaded an American tourist, just a week before I arrived in Davao City, and were launching frequent attacks on shopping malls and restaurants. Local terrorism was at its height. At the same time, Southern Mindanao had a child going blind every day from vitamin A deficiency, a leading cause of blindness in children worldwide.

A local Catholic priest frequently went in and out of the jungle to meet with Abu Sayyaf guerillas. I explained to the priest what we were doing on health and nutrition in Davao City and that Muslim children in the jungle were just as susceptible to vitamin A blindness as were Catholic children in the city. Abu Sayyaf parents in the jungle loved their children just as much as Catholic parents in the city, so what was needed was to solve this mutual problem to prevent childhood blindness and prevent more bloodshed. I proposed going into the jungle with the priest on his next trip to meet with Abu Sayyaf guerillas. He agreed.

Public health affects both sides in a conflict and can therefore be a path to mutual understanding and peace. Even in defense, the Rondine Method can be applied to resolve conflict. What is needed is going beyond traditional interventions and reforming defense policies and programs, just as reforming development and diplomacy is needed. Again, the Rondine Method has proven itself in diplomacy, and what is true for diplomacy is also true for development and defense. Let's focus on what we know to be true.

The Way Forward

The world has entered something of a perfect storm when it comes to foreign affairs. Government instability, corruption, terrorism, refugees, hunger, disease, and environmental devastation are all increasing even as funding for international crises is decreasing. If we are to have any chance of addressing the growing crises worldwide, more efficient, more effective, and more sustainable diplomacy, development, and defense are needed.

Current foreign policy has also created poor diplomacy in the face of growing nationalism worldwide. As funding for international development dries up, a foreign aid mafia, made up of large, bureaucratic aid organizations, government agencies, and powerful corporations dictate how foreign aid is done and by whom. Finally, a worldwide military industrial complex perpetuates, rather than prevents, war.

As noted, for development, only a small fraction of donated money gets into affected countries and to affected populations. Many foreign interventions end as soon as funding runs out, and many international aid organizations have been accused of being more concerned with their own program budgets than solving problems in the affected countries.

What is needed is true, foreign aid reform—using the Rondine Method— which allows locally led interventions in diplomacy, development, and defense that operate from the bottom up, instead of the top down, and from the inside out, instead of the outside in. As stated, these locally led interventions actually cost less, react quicker, and are far more effective and more sustainable than expensive interventions led by New York, Washington, and Geneva. Locally led interventions, managed by faith-based organizations, colleges and universities, and NGOs in-country also build independence and self-sufficiency in-country, rather than dependence on foreign assistance. What's more, these locally led interventions build good public relations for donor countries because more money gets into the affected population, rather than into the pockets of private contractors and large, international aid organizations. In this way, countries can solve their own problems, rather than relying on the international community to solve their problems for them.

"It's the Approach, Stupid"

To paraphrase President Clinton's campaign slogan from the 1990s, it's the *approach* to foreign relations that needs to be reformed. How we *manage* foreign policy is the problem, not the availability of resources, funding, or technology. We can solve many of the global crises occurring throughout the world today if we simply manage foreign policy smarter. But for that to occur, poor countries need to take an active and equal role with wealthy countries in that reform.

If the twenty-first-century economy is any indication, we need to *cut out the middleman* and let affected parties confer directly. The increase in crises and worldwide decline in funding only make this management decision more urgent. We know there is a better way: the Rondine way. We just need to follow what we know to be true.

Conclusion

More needs to be understood about the Rondine Method being applied to the 3Ds and working from the bottom up, instead of the top down, and from the inside out, instead of the outside in. Although it may be completely contrary to current foreign policy as we know it, Colonial aid programs as we have today are unsustainable and more likely to create resentment, rather than respect—war rather than peace.

Done correctly, diplomacy, development, and defense reform can be a rallying cry to attract even more funding for crises occurring throughout the world, but foreign interventions need to be more effective, more immediate, and more sustainable than the Colonial aid and defense programs we have witnessed for the last one hundred years, which are more likely to create dependence, rather than independence.

The Rondine Method can be used to solve conflicts between wealthy donor countries and poor recipient countries simply by listening to local problems, being more responsive to local needs, and acting locally. As noted, the goal is to help countries and communities solve their own problems, rather than solving their problems for them.

If we truly expect to see self-determination, peace, and prosperity throughout the world, we must enable local residents by providing them with the tools, training, and technology and act as friends and coaches so local residents can train and educate one another. We cannot wait for the next international crisis to occur. We must prepare now. The Rondine Method is the bridge to understanding and the right way to conduct foreign policy and the 3Ds.

Understand that it is how we *manage* diplomacy, development, and defense that is the problem, not the availability of resources. More effective foreign policy can be accomplished simply by providing better communication, already available resources, and the know-how to allow countries to solve their own problems. All they need is a little coaching. Foreign governments, corporations, foundations, universities, faith-based organizations, and NGOs must be seen as peers—not saviors—to allow local residents to launch their own interventions, benefiting developed and undeveloped countries alike. The goal is more equal, more honest, and more effective foreign relations.

Maybe Rondine is three-dimensional after all, and the rest of the world is still thinking one-dimensionally?

Note

1. Foreign aid reform was a concept started by Professor Kaiser in the 1990s and represents a culmination of his thirty-plus years developing better foreign interventions in especially problematic countries.

CHAPTER 8

The Rondine Method and Creative Conflict Transformation

INSIGHTS FROM CONTACT THEORY AND INTERRELIGIOUS PEACEBUILDING

Gerard Powers

The Rondine Method represents one form of implementing contact theory. In its simplest formulation, contact theory assumes that an important means of conflict resolution, peacebuilding, and reconciliation is to bring together individuals from "enemy" communities to better understand each other, find common ground, and build relationships that can overcome hatred, fear, and demonization of the Other. Rondine's approach is somewhat distinctive in that it emphasizes long-term engagement in a safe environment that promotes honest dialogue and the development of trusting friendships. And these friendships are meant to be sustained and bear fruit through working together for peace long after the students return to their home country.

This chapter will, first, consider how Rondine's approach to conflict transformation through interpersonal engagement fits with findings from contact theory. Given that many Rondine students come from conflicts with a strong religious dimension, this chapter will then consider how Rondine's method relates to insights from interreligious peacebuilding.

Rondine Method, Conflict Transformation, and Contact Theory

Programs based on a contact theory of peacebuilding have proliferated for decades. Studies have shown that the quantity and quality of contact are critical for programs to reduce prejudice and lead to greater support for peacebuilding (McKeown and Taylor 2017, 426). The Rondine Method is creative in that it relies on a far more sophisticated, deep, and long-term approach than is typical of many such programs. Rondine does not assume that building relationships across deep communal divides will automatically lead to positive change in attitudes or sustainable, positive interpersonal relationships. Rather, its leaders understand that contact theory works only if these relationships are carefully cultivated over a long period of time with considerable professional facilitation to help address the inevitable "stops" along the way. Rondine understands that overcoming the fear, pain, and hatred involved in the construction of "the enemy" requires a long-term, intentional, guided process that is perhaps akin to the process of trauma healing.

Rondine's key concepts of using hospitality and dialogue to build trust and friendship amidst difference evoke themes central to the encyclical *Fratelli tutti*. Pope Francis defines *fraternity* as social friendship and a culture of encounter. What he says about the option for the poor reflects what might be called Rondine's option for the enemy: "The option for the poor should lead us to friendship with the poor" because it is the only way to understand their values, desires, ways of living their faith (Pope Francis 2020, 221). Rondine tries to experience the authority that comes from the fragile, from conditions of vulnerability, from victims and fringes. The ability to grasp the stories of the pain of others, beyond the ritual, requiring telling of one's own, already takes a tiny step outside the closed boundary and the mechanisms of simplification and dehumanization (Vaccari 2018c). It does so by creating what Pope Francis calls "processes of encounter, processes that build a people that can accept differences" of cultures and worldviews (Pope Francis 2020, 217). Rondine's process of encounter foregrounds hospitality to strangers. As Miguel Díaz (2019) notes, "embracing [Rondine's] practice of hospitality—a personal and daily commitment to inclusive and just accompaniment—offers a hope that it is possible to overcome poisonous discourse and violent actions that divide our human family." Rondine's emphasis on developing friendships is similar to the approach of the Community of Sant'Egidio, renowned for facilitating formal peace processes and its interfaith engagement, which considers hospitality and friendship as central to its identity and work (Johnston 2008).

An important character trait that Rondine tries to cultivate is compassion for the enemy. Daniel Rothbart and Susan Allen, in a study of Rondine's Method, noted two elements of compassion: a sense of sympathy for the other's suffering and a sense of hope that the person's suffering will end and the person will thrive. Rothbart and Allen (2019) explain how conflict transformation works:

> [C]onflict actors resist the social psychological forces of defining their adversaries in terms of their inherent viciousness, inhumanity, and lust for violence. These are the forces of categorical difference in moralistic attributes that seem fixed in the bedrock of the social–political order. When genuine transformation is achieved, conflict actors humanize their adversaries as complex beings who experience

a wide range of emotions, from love of family members to fears of the enemy at the gate, and who face similar challenges regarding the deprivation of the basic needs.

Put another way, conflict transformation is possible because individuals are capable of viewing the enemy with the necessary moral nuance that rejects any inferences of collective guilt.

One way to escape the social–psychological and moral prison of collective guilt is to celebrate cases of courageous acts of compassion to protect the Other who is victimized. During World War II, "Righteous Gentiles" risked their lives to save Jews. One study found that most of these people shared a deep ethical commitment to care for those in danger because of their inherent human dignity, not because of religious motivations (Al Ramiah and Hewstone 2013). In the case of the Hutus who helped save people during the Rwandan genocide, compassion for the suffering of others and Christian convictions were prominent motivators. Celebrating courageous acts of the Other has its limitations. A Jewish victim of the Holocaust or a Tutsi victim of Hutu militias might readily acknowledge the heroic acts of some Germans or some Hutus but dismiss them as simply heroic exceptions that prove the rule, that most Germans or Hutus were complicit in genocide. So, too, a Rondine student who has developed a close friendship with an "enemy" and came to a common commitment to work together for peace when they return home might continue to believe that the fellow student is not typical of their community but is the heroic peacebuilder exception. If that is the case, the relationships formed at Rondine might not significantly affect a student's view of the enemy group as a whole.

That is why experts in contact theory suggest that those involved in programs such as Rondine's need to be sufficiently typical of the communities from which they come. As Al Ramiah and Hewstone (2013) conclude, "Research strongly supports the roles of group salience and perceived typicality in promoting the generalization of contact effects beyond the immediate interpersonal contact situation to the outgroup as a whole." Therefore, the impact of Rondine's method will depend, at least in part, on the extent to which the participants are, and are perceived to be, representative of their respective religious, ethnic, or national groups.

Research also suggests that the generalization of contact effects also depends on whether a student is from a minority or majority group. Again, Al Ramiah and Hewstone (2013) conclude that a review of studies shows that "positive intergroup contact reduced the symbolic threat that minority group members perceived from the majority group, which was associated with more positive evaluations of the majority group" (533). The effects were less evident among members of the majority group, however, because symbolic threats were less salient to them because their political power enabled them to more easily protect their identity from the minority's threats.

That disparate effect between members of minority and majority groups highlights a larger factor. Conflicts are highly complex. Prejudice or hatred of another group is only one of many factors involved in a conflict. So programs that mainly address prejudice or hatred of members of another group only address one aspect of the conflict and could deflect attention and action from more systemic issues. Rondine promotes a "culture of coexistence" based on the contention that "interpersonal relationships are stronger than borders" (Vaccari 2018c, 296). Rondine students might return home with less prejudice and hatred toward the Other, but their view of the overall conflict and possibilities for peacebuilding might not change significantly. For example, a Catholic Republican from Northern Ireland might return home from Rondine with less prejudice toward Protestant Unionists and might even see both Catholics and Protestants as victims of conflict. But the Catholic Republican might continue to believe that the fundamental problem is British colonialism and the only solution is a united Ireland. Similarly, their Protestant Unionist colleague, much more able to empathize with and respect Catholics, might feel equally strongly that continued union with Britain was the only way forward.

Rondine's method helps address this risk that interpersonal relationship-building deflects attention from the need for systemic change by ensuring that students look at the conflict in which they are embroiled through a wider lens of conflict resolution, peacebuilding, and reconciliation. Rondine understands that conflict transformation requires work at many levels by many different actors to address many different factors. Its efforts at changing individual hearts and minds is one element of the conflict transformation theory of change. Numerous studies have shown that intergroup contact programs like Rondine are effective in reducing prejudice, anxiety, and a sense of threat and increasing empathy and trust. According to McKeown and Taylor (2017), "[T]hese factors may be important antecedents and precursors of support for peacebuilding, which in turn, may motivate further action to help reconstruct society after conflict" (416).

The strength of the Rondine Method is that it contains key elements that research shows are necessary for intergroup contact programs to contribute to conflict resolution. Al Ramiah and Hewstone (2013) summarize these as follows:

- The students have equal status; they have deep interpersonal interactions over a long period of time.
- The program targets the main psychological processes behind the beneficial effects of contact.
- The students' interactions are linked to their respective groups so that there can be group salience; interactions are oriented toward a common goal.

- There is strong institutional support (schools are particularly good at this), and the participants are sufficiently typical of their group.

The Rondine Method and Interreligious Peacebuilding

Rondine brings together individuals on opposite sides of communal divides that, in many cases, are defined, at least in part, by religious identities. Given the religious dimension to the identity conflicts from which many students have come, Rondine, like many other programs, is engaged in a form of interreligious peacebuilding. What is creative is how Rondine addresses the religious dimensions of communal divides through a sophisticated psychological and philosophical approach. This section identifies issues that arise in interreligious dialogue and peacebuilding that are relevant to the Rondine method.

Like contact theory, more generally, interreligious peacebuilding typically has one or more of the following distinct but often related purposes: (1) deepening relationships (dialogue of life), (2) improving understanding (dialogue of words), (3) finding common ground on beliefs (dialogue of spirituality/faith), and (4) promoting common or complementary action (Neufeldt 2016; Lederach et al. 2007). The Rondine Method devotes much of its attention to what arguably are the two most challenging elements of interreligious peacebuilding: the dialogue of life and the dialogue of words. It uses those elements as a foundation for a dialogue of spirituality/faith and a dialogue of action. The dialogues of life and words are grounded in an affective theory of change that posits that peace is built by transforming sectarian *communal* relationships by means of a long, slow process of building strong *interpersonal* relationships, which promotes peace by changing the hearts and minds of participants about the conflict and each other. Rondine brings together those who are eager to know each other "in the flesh," to oust enmity and seek friendships that can overcome sectarian divides. These relationships become "stable in dialogue" through three steps that can involve spirituality and faith: the first discovers common ground, the second accepts the "different aspects," and the third acknowledges the limits of mutual understanding (Vaccari 2018c, 264–65). The relationships and understanding forged at Rondine lay the foundation for a dialogue of action whereby its graduates find ways to cooperate across communal divides when they return to their home countries.

Interreligious peacebuilding often suffers from a paradox: the more religion is central to a conflict, the greater the need for interreligious peacebuilding; the less religion is central to the conflict, the greater the likelihood that interreligious peacebuilding will bear fruit. Therefore, interreligious engagement has to be based on a clear theory of change and must address several challenges that arise in interreligious dialogue and peacebuilding that also arise with the Rondine Method. In pursuing a dialogue of action when they return to their home countries, graduates of Rondine must decide whether they will work for peace primarily within their own community (single identity peacebuilding) or work primarily through joint initiatives across the communal divides (interreligious peacebuilding), which seems to be the priority of the Rondine Method. Both kinds of work are necessary, and they should relate to each other. But each has its own dynamics and distinct advantages and disadvantages.

First, just as most interreligious dialogues involve moderates, Rondine brings together those who are eager to know the Other and to return to their countries and work together for intercommunal dialogue, peace, and reconciliation. This is partly making a virtue of necessity—extremists are likely to view dialogue as entailing illegitimate compromise or risking their own status—and partly a well-established strategy—moderates can strengthen their voice and legitimacy in ways that can help them marginalize the extremists in their midst. Engaging moderates from the "enemy" community is often easier than engaging extremists within one's own community. Here I differ with Marc Gopin (2000, 48), who claims it is easier to convince someone to engage in peacebuilding from within one's own community than it is to engage in authentic dialogue with one's adversary. Engaging moderates enhances prospects for effective common or complementary action and avoids giving legitimacy to those who misuse religion to foment division and violence. But it also limits the effectiveness of dialogue because those most responsible for the violence are not engaged and often actively oppose interreligious dialogue and common action (Banchoff 2008, 67). When they return home, Rondine students might feel that they are reinforcing communal conflicts if they do not engage in cross-communal dialogue and peacebuilding. Yet if they do, they might be dismissed by members of their own community as no better than traitors. They can face resistance and conflict with family, friends, and colleagues within their own community while the conflict dynamics in the wider society might make it difficult to maintain the cross-communal relationships they cultivated at Rondine (Vaccari 2018c, 232).

Second, in conflicts with a strong religious dimension, one is faced with the question of whether dialogue should focus on common ground or differences in religious and ethical beliefs. Interestingly, in many conflicts with a religious dimension, formal interreligious dialogues on religious beliefs often are separate from interreligious dialogues on peace and justice issues. This separation between dialogue around doctrine and dialogue around peacebuilding is due, in part, to a desire not to allow political conflicts to sidetrack doctrinal dialogues and, in part, to a conviction that the long-term process of resolving doctrinal differences will have little impact on conflicts, which, while having a religious dimension, are often not about religious beliefs and teachings. Focusing on religious beliefs can be helpful in identifying common commitments to the sacredness of human life, the obligation to seek the common good of all, and the rejection of religious violence.

But such a focus can divert attention to other issues that divide religious communities, such as differing assessments of the nature of the conflict and possible solutions. Moreover, a focus on finding common ground on religious beliefs leads to a least-common-denominator approach that emasculates the richness and distinctiveness of the Muslim, Christian, Hindu, or indigenous traditions, thereby reducing the ability of faith to motivate and inspire ordinary believers to be peacebuilders. For example, the sacrament of reconciliation can be a powerful motivation for Catholics to seek interpersonal and communal forgiveness, but an effort to find a common religious understanding of reconciliation among Catholics, Protestants, Muslims, Hindus, and indigenous peoples could be a source of unnecessary division and divert time, resources, and attention from pursuing collaborative or complementary action on matters more directly tied to the conflict. Moreover, in conflicts where religious and communal identities are inseparable, efforts to deemphasize what is distinctive in one's own religious tradition can exacerbate the problem of what Gopin calls "negative identity," the tendency to define one's religion in opposition to the "other" (Gopin 2000, 62–64). Therefore, interreligious peacebuilding, at its best, does not seek to minimize the importance of distinctive religious identities but rather, seeks to find within those identities distinctive resources for peacebuilding.

Third, Rondine selects students based on their willingness and potential to return to their conflicted countries and work together across communal divides for dialogue and reconciliation. Rondine sets aside the criteria commonly used for dialogue in situations of conflict—whether informal dialogues of religious leaders and civil society to dialogues of states. The Rondine International Peace Lab supports Ambassadors of Peace and Reconciliation, who embrace a "new style" that is not based on traditional patterns of representation based on national, ethnic, cultural, or religious identity but rather, exclusively on the pillars of mutual trust and competence.

Rondine's Method, therefore, is not based primarily on finding common ground on religious beliefs or the nature of the conflict or possible solutions as much as it is based on the quality of relationships—friendships!—forged at Rondine. It envisions Rondine graduates playing a mediator role: placing themselves in a hospitable relationship with both parties and reinforcing themselves as a "healthy carrier of friendship" (Vaccari 2018c, 239). For example, Azerbaijani and Armenian graduates hosted a camp for youth from both sides. Graduates from Sierra Leone organized a campaign in support of peaceful democratic elections not based on tribal identity.

Rondine's approach has much in common with interreligious peacebuilding, which seeks to overcome mistrust and misunderstandings, to deepen relationships that can bridge the communal divide, to find common ground, and to take at least symbolic common actions to counter the extremists who preach religious conflict. But the purpose and benefit of the kind of interreligious engagement done at Rondine might not be common action but rather, what the coming together allows each student to do within their own community. In many conflict situations, common action on the part of religious actors might be difficult because of the depth of the communal divide as well as its impact being limited. So complementary action is often more effective. Rondine devotes the time, resources, and professional expertise necessary to assist participants in making the very difficult transition from the safe and artificial environment of Rondine to the treacherous reality of the conflicts in their homelands. Where sectarian realities back home make it extremely difficult to sustain their interpersonal friendships, that interpersonal relationship will likely continue to bear fruit in what it allows each individual to do within their own community. Because of the hard work of building relationships at Rondine, they are able to engage in a countercultural narrative that helps their own community better understand "the enemy." As with interreligious dialogue, their Rondine dialogue enables them to go back and work within their own community to help it break out of its myths of unique victimization, to counter stereotypes and prejudices, and to promote better understanding and respect for the hopes and fears and legitimate grievances of the other community. A major test for the Rondine Method over time will be to determine whether its methods enhance the ability of its "moderate" graduates to draw on their improved understanding of the Other, as well as what is distinctive in their own tradition, to engage and/or counter more effectively the extremists in their own community.

Fourth, because interreligious peacebuilding is prone to a least-common-denominator approach, it also lacks some of the power of single identity peacebuilding. In some of the world's most devastating and long-standing conflicts, such as Colombia and the Democratic Republic of Congo, religion plays a key role in peacebuilding, but the conflict does not have a significant religious dimension. The remarkable political and social transformations in Poland, East Germany, the Philippines, and Serbia were influenced by a single dominant religion, often with close ties to national identity. Peacebuilding within one's own community can draw on the full complement of a tradition's rituals, beliefs, norms, spirituality, and communal identity, which is not possible even in the most effective interreligious peacebuilding. Even in conflicts with a religious dimension, extremists within a religious tradition will most likely be marginalized not because the moderates are engaged in interreligious initiatives but because the moderates can appeal to their own rich set of religious resources to convince their co-religionists that extremism is antithetical to their tradition. In short, interreligious peacebuilding is sometimes essential and effective, but it is often not the most essential and effective form of religious peacebuilding.

Conclusion

Peace is a complex puzzle, a continual work in progress involving many factors and actors at many levels using many different means to achieve a vision of reconciliation and a just peace. Rondine is one piece of that complex puzzle. It takes a sophisticated and long-term approach to individual and interpersonal healing, reconciliation, and peacebuilding by bringing together individuals from across conflict divides. It is an effort to meet a need Pope Francis identified in his address to Rondine, which we included as the foreword to this book. "There is a need," Pope Francis said, "for leaders with a new mentality . . . a leader who does not try to meet the "enemy," to sit with him at the table as you do, cannot lead his people to peace." Rondine is developing that kind of leader through its creative version of contact theory. Like interreligious peacebuilding, it is cultivating intangible changes in people, relationships, and values with a long-term horizon. Its success is, by definition, inherently difficult to measure, but the need it is filling is indisputable.

CHAPTER 9

The Rondine Method
BUILDING PEACE THROUGH COMPASSION[1]

Daniel Rothbart and Susan Allen

Hatred, fear, repulsion, antagonism, and humiliation—these emotions inten-
sify enmity between actors of many protracted violent conflicts. Such enmity
is fueled by storytelling practices about the enemy's actions, character traits,
and schemes for conquest, all of which generate a sense of the Other as mortal
enemy. The narratives of enmity tend to follow a familiar pattern:

> Our adversaries have harmed our people.
> They will continue to harm our people.
> They are all bad and will always be bad.
> We are perennial targets of their malice.
> They represent existential threats to us—our mortal enemy.

In the heat of violence, such a pattern can overwhelm the collective consciousness of conflict actors. With such consciousness, the world is reduced to
fabricated and fixed divisions between right and wrong actions, virtuous and
vicious character traits, and good and bad people. These divisions foster crystal-
ized categories of "their" evil and "our" purity. As the complexity of each human
being is suppressed from such categories, so, too, is their humanity.

The Rondine Method seeks to break this downward spiral of enmity by tap-
ping into something fundamentally human. This is the psychological drive and
need to foster bonds, not breaks; cooperation, not competition; and pro-social
feelings of others, even of those affiliated with the enemy camp. In particular,
the inducement of compassion goes to the core of the Rondine Method as a
productive means for conflict prevention.

In this chapter, we explore the centrality of compassion practices to the field of
peacebuilding generally. Going beyond the obvious psychological point that many
individual practitioners in this field are personally motivated by their compassion for
the suffering of vulnerable population groups, we argue that certain forms of practice

give primacy to the norm of compassion. Such practices are supported by recent findings in moral psychology about the nature of sympathy, empathy, and compassion for others. In particular, psychologists have documented that such emotions can be induced in ways that prompt positive, pro-social interactions.

Our objective is not to correct conflict resolution practices per se. We seek, rather, to reflect upon and promote certain forms of compassion-motivated practices. We begin with a case study of one peacebuilding initiative regarding the conflict between Georgians and South Ossetians. After summarizing certain critical developments in experimental psychology about compassion, we examine three forms of peacebuilding practices that give prominence to promoting compassion among the conflict actors. These practices center on (1) the human rights agenda as adopted by the United Nations; (2) certain bottom-up practices of everyday peacemaking of civilians who are caught in the tumult of violent conflict; and (3) the practices of conflict resolution facilitators who engage representatives of conflict parties in interactive conflict resolution. Regarding interactive conflict resolution, we offer four forms of constructive dialogue in which compassion is a tacit norm of interaction among participants. We conclude with recommendations for enhancing compassion-related practices generally.

With this reflective analysis on peacebuilding, we draw upon the notion of systemic compassion as critical to conflict resolution. This notion may seem odd. How can we talk about systems of any emotion? In response, we note that social scientists have examined the systems of negative emotions as a causal source of violent behavior. Consider the social systems of hatred fostered in propaganda campaigns preceding episodes of genocidal violence and the systems of fear generated by demagogues to exploit the passions of vulnerable population groups. So why not probe the systems of positive emotions? In general, systemic compassion refers to the socially sanctioned patterns of practice in a field that privileges the norm of compassion as an organizing principle. That is, such a norm motivates and gives meaning to certain peacebuilding practices. Underpinning our argument is the notion that a mode of practice is a tendency or disposition to act in certain ways within a particular sphere of social activities, called a field (Bourdieu 1977, 85–87). For example, the professions of health care, humanitarian relief, and economic development establish compassion for the suffering of others as a defining norm. These professions of systemic compassion recognize that a certain population group is situated within their circle of moral concern. So, too, with conflict resolution.

Case Study

An example of compassion practices in international conflict resolution can be found in the workshops that focused on the conflict over South Ossetia. This conflict is part of a web of interrelated conflicts. We focus on the Georgian–South Ossetian relationship and the role of compassion in Georgian–South Ossetian conflict resolution practices.

What is involved in the Georgian–South Ossetian relationship? The crux of their contentious relationship centers on the status of South Ossetia, which Georgians see as part of Georgia. South Ossetians recognize their region as an independent country. Several clearly contrasting stories can be identified as dominant, yet competing, narratives. The contrasting views considered here are stereotypical Georgian, Abkhaz, South Ossetian, and Russian viewpoints. Clearly, not all individuals in the ethnic groups will or do see things with the respective stereotypical views described below. However, these views provide a sense of the extreme divergence of narratives and are, therefore, useful in contextualizing the more nuanced, complex understandings of the conflicts at play.

Relationships between political units form the basis for many of the conflictual narratives and viewpoints between the parties. Georgians tend to operate within the collective memory of a history of oppression by Russia, often describing their relationship with the metaphor of Russia as a big bear to the north of much smaller Georgia and seeing that bear as a hungry intruder in Georgia today. Georgian President Mikheil Saakashvili stated that Russia "is dreaming about how to abolish Georgia's sovereignty" (Saakashvili 2008). Juxtaposed against this is an Abkhaz view of Georgian oppression of the less numerous Abkhaz people, reflected in the image of then president of Georgia Zviad Gamsakhurdia calling for "Georgia for the Georgians" in 1991 Similarly, South Ossetians also speak of Georgian oppression of the less numerous. South Ossetian people, along with a relatively fresh memory of betrayal, when Georgian President Mikheil Saakashvili reassured residents of South Ossetia that he had instructed the Georgian military and police not to return fire on the evening of August 7, 2008, just before more intensive fighting began that very night (Saakashvili 2008). On the Russian side, there is an understanding of Russian intervention as a beneficial and necessary process toward protecting Abkhaz, South Ossetians, and also Russian citizens from Georgian attack. This view resonates with South Ossetian Eduard Kokoity's praising Russian prime minister Vladimir Putin: "decisions you have taken saved a whole nation from extermination" (BBC 2009). Of course, this view contrasts sharply with the Georgian view, which sees Russia first as an invading and now an occupying force.

Through the activation of compassion in conflict resolution processes, these differing goals do lend themselves to the discovery of at least one common vision, which is inherently humanitarian. This vision includes a realization of shared, concrete human interests, such as having a home and access to water, being healthy, connecting with friends and family, and being gainfully employed. This vision provides a goal for cooperation across the conflict divide in efforts to open these opportunities to people who suffered from war and war's long-term effects. Cooperation to care for an urgently ill child or to repair a broken dam can provide an impetus for working across the conflict divide toward nonpolitical humanitarian goals.

After the August 2008 war, the first Georgian–South Ossetian Civil Society workshop, which gathered at George Mason University's Point of View conflict resolution retreat facility opened with a simple question: Is there anything to talk about after the war? There were two main topics of conversation: explaining to each other their experiences of the recent war and working together to find ways to address the humanitarian needs that remain in the months after the war. Sharing stories of the war activated compassion, as everyone listened attentively to each person's recollection of those terrifying days. People exhibited sympathy for the suffering that participants recounted. Some cried.

Once compassion had been activated through such storytelling in the first workshop, the subsequent workshops, which extended for years, centered on humanitarian needs. First, the workshops took the form of problem-solving workshops. Georgians and South Ossetians worked together on humanitarian issues, such as repairing a broken dam that might have flooded both South Ossetian and Georgian villages, working on access to gas and to irrigation water, expediting health care access for emergencies that require crossing the ceasefire line to reach the nearest hospital, and arranging the simultaneous release of multiple prisoners from across the conflict divides. Over the years, Georgians and South Ossetians made progress on these issues in many future workshops. These conversations in the interactive conflict resolution context were motivated by compassion.

Eventually the Georgian–South Ossetian problem-solving workshops became "catalytic workshops," which precipitated other confidence-building measures. Once other confidence-building measures were well underway, the workshops took on a form of sustained dialogue. With the sustained dialogue model, a core group of peacebuilders from across the ceasefire line meet to maintain direct constructive communication and the deep understanding of the other perspectives that develop with such discussion. By meeting periodically, the participants maintain their compassionate understanding of experience on the other side of the ceasefire line.

How has compassion been engaged in other aspects of the Georgian–South Ossetian relationship? Compassion has been a part of the few successes in the official diplomacy at the Geneva international discussions, where quarterly talks regularly focus on issues of protocol and recognition and often result in walkouts by the Abkhaz and Ossetian participants. However, after interactive conflict resolution workshops considered the repair of a broken dam, the ability of ambulances to cross the ceasefire line, and the possibilities for simultaneous release of specific prisoners, the humanitarian issues section of the Geneva talks led to agreements on these humanitarian actions. Even the official diplomats reached agreement on certain actions.

Considering more grassroots conflict resolution practices, compassion has been a major component of the Georgian–South Ossetian women's dialogues, which reunite women who had been former neighbors. Following one dialogue, a mother from one side of the ceasefire line was reunited with her daughter from the other side. The women could not cross the ceasefire line to see each other but traveled separate routes to Yerevan, where they were reunited. While contact across the ceasefire line has at times been discouraged by the South Ossetian leadership, a reunion between a mother and her daughter could not be discouraged out of compassion for that family bond that had been challenged by the war and that resulted in fragmentation of the population.

The Psychology of Compassion

Social psychologists have recognized compassion as a distinct emotional state along with affinities to sympathy, empathy, pity, hope, desire, and caring. Typically, an experience of compassion is neither momentary, like a pinprick, nor superficial, like one's desire for chocolate cake. Compassion is recognized as a distinct psychological state regarding the plight of others. This state consists of two elements. First, with compassion, one experiences a sensitivity to the pain or suffering of other persons and, second, one experiences a deep desire to alleviate that suffering either through one's own actions or through the actions of others. Underpinning this desire is an apprehension of the present suffering of a person and the hope for relief of their troubles. For example, one might experience compassion upon witnessing someone with severe bodily injury, hearing the pleas of children begging on the street, or reading stories of devastation of refugees who are forced to flee from their homes to avoid the ravages of war. While research psychologists do not believe that compassion represents an innate, inborn drive, they have shown that some individuals are routinely more kind, helpful, and willing to sacrifice their goods for others. The notion of a compassionate personality has garnered considerable empirical support (Bierhoff, Klein, and Kramp 1991; Galston 1993; Krebs and Van Hesteren 1992; Oliner and Oliner 1988).

But compassion does not always prompt action. One can experience a desire for the relief of others' suffering without acting as an agent of such relief. Moreover, compassion comes with a sense of possession. To experience compassion implies that I "have" it as "my" own. But such possession is not like having a kneecap, which always comes with me whether I am interacting with others or not. Compassion is a social enterprise, promoting a sense of bonding with others.

Importantly, researchers have shown that compassion can be induced for some people under certain specific conditions. One method of inducement developed by a team of psychologists is called Cognitively Based Compassion Training (CBCT)

(Ozawa-de Silva et al. 2012). With this method, research subjects undergo several days of training. Subsequently, they tend to help others at a higher rate in comparison to those who were not given compassion training (Fredrickson et al. 2008). In other studies, such inducement consisted in meditation training. The calmness that is prompted by meditation gave rise to feelings of interconnection with those who are thought to be suffering, even if they are strangers (Lutz et al. 2008).

Moreover, experimental psychologists have correlated the inducement of compassion with changes in neuro-processing. Psychologists use the term *neuroplasticity* to refer to the functions of the adult brain that can be altered through sustained practice (Klimecki 2015). For example, in one study, twenty students were shown pictures of people suffering from the effects of living under dire conditions. After viewing the slides, the students were asked to rate the overall intensity of their emotional response to the sequence of pictures. Students were then subjected to fMRI scanning to determine their neurological responses. The studies revealed patterns of neural activity that correlated strongly with the experiences of induced compassion. Their neural networks associated with positive (pro-social) affect were activated (Klimecki et al. 2014).

Neuroscientific studies reveal a significant difference between an experience of compassion and that of empathy. An experience of empathy was shown to activate certain neural networks that are known to be associated with physical pain. In controlled experiments, members of one group were exposed to actual physical pain, and those of another group were exposed to films that evoked a sense of shared emotion—empathy—to those who exhibited extreme suffering. The portions of the brain that were activated for both groups of participants were the same, that is, the anterior insula and the anterior middle cingulate cortex. These findings were confirmed when participants underwent empathy training for several days, which revealed, through fMRI examination, that the portions of the brain associated with negative emotional feelings—insula and anterior middle cingulate cortex— were activated. With empathy, experimental subjects sought to withdraw from the scene of suffering.

Motivated by these findings in moral psychology, we turn to the field of peacebuilding, focusing on three domains where compassion practices are exhibited.

Compassion Practice in International Humanitarian Law: Case of the United Nations

Moving from experimental psychology to peacebuilding, we find that the norm of compassion has primacy in the human rights agenda of international law. Consider, for example, the principle of human dignity adopted by the United Nations, according to which all humans are born with inherent moral worth and bestowed with certain inalienable rights. Included in the Universal Declaration of Human Rights (UDHR) is the following ontological claim: "All members of the human family are born with dignity, equality and inalienable rights" (Preamble, Universal Declaration of Human Rights). In like measure, Articles 1, 22, and 23 of the UDHR include the claim that each person—whether one is president or pauper, slave or slave master—is endowed with rights by virtue of being human, regardless of life conditions, social status, financial resources, or capacity to influence others. Such rights are obviously inseparable from one's humanity as birth rights (Beyleveld and Brownsword 1998; Dicke 2002; Donnelly 1982). With dignity, each person deserves respect for their human rights; UDHR is grounded morally on the claim of universal dignity.

In the formative stages of crafting the UDHR, the principle of universal dignity was advanced by Jacques Maritain, a philosopher who served as a primary drafter of the UDHR. He argued that dignity goes to the core of human existence and that all member states of the UN should be responsible for the suffering of vulnerable population groups. Maritain was not alone. Eleanor Roosevelt, who chaired the UN Human Rights Commission, accepted the primacy of human dignity. She claimed that the world of human rights is the world of the individual person, where "every man, woman, and child seek equal justice, equal opportunity, equal dignity without discrimination" (Romany 1994, 90).

The advocates of realist models of international relations tend to reject the human rights agenda as a utopian image that fosters distortions of the real-world complexities of war and peace. Yet this objection to the human rights agenda of the UDHR reflects a serious misunderstanding. While the agenda is moralistic, it does not transcend the realities of war. In fact, the UDHR includes an imperative to investigate the realism of systemic vulnerability of certain categories of people (Engle Merry 2007, 195). Such an imperative calls for the sympathetic understanding of those population groups who are prone to suffer during and after war, conjoined with the institutional imperative to mitigate such suffering. The 1951 UN Convention on the Prevention and Punishment of the Crime of Genocide recognizes the vulnerability of "national, ethnical, racial or religious groups." The UN International Covenant on Civil and Political Rights, adopted in 1966, recognizes "ethnic, religious or linguistic minorities" as vulnerable groups. And women are recognized in the 1979 Convention on the Elimination of All Forms of Discrimination against Women.

So the UDHR establishes compassion as a primary norm for a sympathetic understanding for vulnerable population groups and the need for mitigating or preventing their suffering.

Compassion as a Norm of Everyday Peace

A second form of compassion practice in peacebuilding centers on the small-scale activities of civilians engulfed in the tumult of large-scale violence. Such activities fall within the domain of everyday peace, reflecting an emic perspective to peacebuilding (Berents 2015; Mac Ginty and Firchow 2016). Every peace centers on actions that are drawn from a community's ethos regarding present imperatives and a vision of the future (Bar-Tal 2013, 174). As Roger Mac Ginty writes, "the everyday is regarded as the normal habitus for individuals and groups, even if what passed as 'normal' in a conflict-affected society would be abnormal elsewhere" (Mac Ginty 2014, 550). The habitus of the everyday rests on core value commitments for determining safe and flourishing communities. Such commitments are central to their sense of in-group identity and out-group difference (Rothbart and Korostelina 2006).

Conflict analysts have gathered evidence about the everyday compassion practices of civilians who are caught in the carnage of mass violence. These practices are illustrated in cases where civilians risk their lives to offer sanctuary to those who are potential victims of violence. For example, during World War II, some civilians offered safety, material goods, and emotional support to Jews. Some rescuers began their activism after being confronted directly with the desperate pleas of Jews. The number of active rescuers during the Nazi occupation of Europe is low, comprising only 0.5 percent of the total civilian population (Oliner and Oliner 1988, 8). But for some of those who did offer sanctuary, their rescue efforts were motivated by strongly held humanitarian values. For example, some rescues were driven by their ethical beliefs that made it imperative to help those in need. Other rescuers grounded their actions in socialist or communist doctrine, which called for resistance against the Nazi invaders (Fogelman 1994, 162–64). Still others were driven by a positive emotional attachment to individual Jews for whom the rescuers had special feelings or love, or to the Jewish people as a whole. The famous case of Oscar Schindler saving Jews illustrates how many Polish rescuers had a special affinity toward Jews (Fogelman 1994, 182–85).

The work of rescuers illustrates collectively oriented compassion. Most rescuers interviewed in one study (87 percent) invoked their deep ethical commitment to care for those in danger, a commitment that was grounded on a belief in universal humanism, a sense of the inherent worth of each person (Oliner and Oliner 1988, 163–64). For a majority of these rescuers, this belief was not driven by their religious convictions, and the rescuers' religious affiliations were not significantly different from those of nonrescuers. Yet the moral imperative to care for those in peril motivated them to save Jews, particularly after witnessing Nazi brutality against them (Suedfeld and De Best 2008, 38–40).

Similar sorts of compassion practices occurred during the genocidal violence in Rwanda in 1994, where Hutu civilians offered safe havens for Tutsis (Rothbart and Cooley 2016). Some Hutus risked their lives trying to rescue Tutsis who were seeking sanctuary, essential material goods, and emotional support. In explaining their actions, most rescuers appealed to their sense of Christian ethics to offer aid to those in need. According to these rescuers, the source of their moral conviction was found in a good heart, which was a physical embodiment of their wisdom to live according to a righteous path, compassion for the suffering of others, and courage to overcome fear and carry out the commands of their faith.

Compassion Practices of Interactive Conflict Resolution

Having considered compassion in international diplomacy and everyday peace, we focus specifically on certain practices of interactive conflict resolution. Interactive conflict resolution has been defined as "conflict analysis or problem-solving discussions in a workshop format that are directed toward mutual understanding of the conflict and the development of collaborative actions to de-escalate and eventually resolve it" (Fisher 1997, 8).

The techniques of interactive conflict resolution center on constructive communication that is guided by both explicit and implicit norms. The explicit norms are conveyed in the rules presented by facilitators during the introductory phase of the workshop, dialogue, or training session. Among these rules, facilitators usually implore participants to maintain confidentiality of statements that are conveyed during the discussion. Participants are also asked to exhibit mutual respect, which in turn is often linked to a sense of caring for the efforts, integrity, and moral worth of others. Compassion practices reflect instrumental norms for constructive communication. The norm of compassion has functional value in contributing to the shared goals of solving problems. This norm can be revealed as participants tell their stories, offer observations, and deliberate over proposals for solving problems. This means–ends value of compassion represents a precondition for constructive dialogue on controversial issues. Yet facilitators should not direct participants explicitly to be compassionate. Facilitators cannot compel, cajole, instruct, or insist that compassion be exhibited in dialogue sessions among adversaries to a conflict. So any participant who exhibits verbal hostility in the form of name-calling, character assassination, or sarcastic ridicule may receive an indirect or direct reprimand from the other participants through a message that such hostility is counterproductive to their collective efforts.

We consider below four forms of interactive conflict resolution: analytical problem-solving workshops, psychodynamic approaches to unofficial diplomacy, sustained dialogue, and trainings that involve dialogue. We focus on the ways in which compassion practices manifest as a core part of each of these conflict resolution practices. Given the psychological findings discussed above that compassion can be induced under certain circumstances, practitioners of interactive conflict resolution are well served to develop compassion, seeking to induce a humanistic-oriented interaction among the workshop participants.

PROBLEM-SOLVING WORKSHOPS

John Burton (1969) developed the problem-solving workshop approach to dialogue in the 1960s and introduced the concept of controlled communication in international relations. Herb Kelman (1972) participated in Burton's second problem-solving workshop in 1966, serving with the social scientists who facilitated the workshop. This workshop focused on Cyprus and was structured around three phases: (1) the participants explained the conflict from each of their perspectives; (2) the social scientists offered models of conflict and helped the participants consider the relevance of these models to the Cyprus conflict; and (3) the participants looked at various ways to resolve the conflict.

Facilitators of problem-solving workshops are expected to take on multiple tasks. Based on Mitchell and Bank's (1996) guide to the problem-solving workshop approach, which Mitchell (2005) expanded, facilitators decide whom to invite, contact the potential participants, explain the process, and make arrangements for the workshop. The workshop itself comprises five sorts of activities. First, it opens with facilitators setting an informal tone and requesting confidentiality. Second, participants are asked to explain the conflict, including its history, present state, and challenges to its resolution. Third, participants and facilitators analyze the conflict by reviewing what was presented in the prior phase, considering relevant conflict theories and considering other conflicts. Fourth, participants consider ways to resolve the conflict or to begin such resolution efforts. Fifth, the facilitators prepare the participants to reenter their home communities and, it is hoped, transfer some of their new insights to their colleagues at home.

Analytical problem-solving gives a central place to compassion. The primary activities of the dialogue session centers on analysis among the workshop participants of the preconditions, causes, and consequences of the hostilities to date. This analysis requires a sympathetic understanding of the perspectives of conflict stakeholders who approach the conflict from different perspectives. In other words, successful analysis requires recognizing each participant's subjectivity. By seeing all participants' perspectives as arising from their experiences (including what their media and leadership have told them), the workshop discussion fosters compassion for the suffering of all involved and respect for different perspectives that are exhibited during the workshop. The ground rules for such dialogue include the following: a commitment to show respect for each other, a demonstration of equal status shown to each participation, and a commitment to maintain confidentiality of statements conveyed during the workshop. In facilitating such dialogue, practitioners seek to change the ways in which the conflict protagonists address their grievances, moving them away from the self-absorption of their hatred of their adversary and toward a humanistic form of interaction that recognizes that all participants arrive at the workshop with different backgrounds and perspectives. With this objective, the practitioners seek to induce among the parties a shift in consciousness about relations with their adversary. According to two conflict resolution mediators, this is a shift in the recognition of the Other "from a negative, destructive, alienating, and demonizing interaction to one that becomes positive, constructive, connecting, and humanizing, even while conflict and disagreement are still continuing" (Bush and Folger 2005, 56). Such a shift fosters sympathetic awareness of shared suffering and an aspiration for relief on both sides. This is a shift from enmity to compassion.

An example of a problem-solving workshop series can be found in the work of the Harvard Study Group, which was structured as a problem-solving workshop series focused on Cyprus. From 1999 to 2003, the Harvard Study Group met seven times, which led to ideas that developed into the Annan Plan. Chigas (2015) describes the problem-solving workshop elements of the Harvard Study Group meetings: "Participants shared their perceptions and concerns, expressed the interests and needs underlying their positions, jointly analyzed the underlying issues, and jointly developed ideas for resolution" (259).

For some problem-solving workshops, the topics discussed are not explicitly focused on the final resolution of the conflict. Consider again the Georgian–South Ossetian workshop series discussed previously. In these workshops, participants jointly developed ideas for confidence-building measures that would support progress toward resolution. To develop appropriate ideas for confidence-building, the participants had to first develop a sympathetic understanding of the perspectives of all who would be involved in confidence-building. What sorts of initiatives would be acceptable on all sides given the subjective experiences of all involved? The workshop participants are not only developing the overall ideas, but they are also working through specific plans for next steps, clarifying who would do what to set each new confidence-building measures in motion. One author of this paper called these workshops "catalytic workshops," highlighting their role in starting up new confidence-building measures (Nan and Greiff 2013).

Compassion is a critical element of productive problem-solving workshops. For any confidence-building program or any overall resolution of the conflict to be successful, the approach must exhibit sympathetic understanding of others.

PSYCHOPOLITICAL DIALOGUE

The skills of psychologists, psychiatrists, and psychoanalysis can also be helpful in interactive conflict resolution. For example, Vamik Volkan (1997) is a psychiatrist who practices psychopolitical dialogue. From such practices, he induces dialogue participants to acquire new insights and to develop action plans and more constructive relationships. Among the many regions in which he practiced, his work in Estonia illustrates his approach. There, Volkan (1997) accompanied Estonian and Russian dialogue participants to various hot spots in Estonia, such as the Paldiski military base, where Russian troops had mostly withdrawn. For Volkan (1997), "A patient's dreams provide access to his unconscious, while visiting hot spots serves a similar function in revealing what otherwise might remain hidden or unexpressed in an intergroup dialogue" (211). Over the course of six years in the 1990s, Volkan and a team convened a series of dialogues with influential individuals in the Estonian and Russian communities in Estonia. The psychological aspects of the dialogues included work with metaphors for the Estonian–Russian relationship and shared analysis as a group of the possibilities for developing that relationship in the future. Concrete initiatives, such as more Estonian language classes for Russian-speaking people in Estonia, were catalyzed by these discussions. The psychopolitical dialogue contributed to conflict prevention in the following respects: attitude impacts on dialogue participants; process impacts on the intermediate processes of conflict resolution in Estonia; and substantive impacts on issues central to the conflict.

Psychodynamic approaches to interactive conflict resolution help develop participants' awareness of their own concerns and those of others. As participants visit hot spots or reflect on flashpoints in current events, they become more aware of their own hidden or unexpressed concerns. Additionally, they reflect upon the other participants' hidden or unexpressed concerns. Then, as in a problem-solving workshop, participants seek to develop specific initiatives to work on those concerns toward resolution of the conflict. These initiatives must address all participants' concerns, which is critical to their success. The psychodynamic approach requires both self-awareness and Other-awareness and the collaborative development of next steps that respond to all participants' concerns.

With the focus on understanding one's own group's concerns and the concerns of other groups, psychodynamic workshops create the basis for and develop compassion. There can be no successful psychodynamic analysis of intergroup conflict without compassion for the groups involved in the conflict.

SUSTAINED DIALOGUE

Harold Saunders (1999) served as a diplomat (Assistant Secretary of State for Near Eastern and South Asian Affairs) and on the National Security Council staff in the Jimmy Carter administration. Saunders participated in the Kissinger shuttle (diplomacy), the Camp David Accords, and the Egyptian–Israeli Peace Treaty. After leaving government service in 1981 at the end of the Carter administration, he joined the Dartmouth Conference, a long-term series of US–Soviet citizen dialogues. From that long experience of governmental and unofficial dialogue, Saunders developed the model of "sustained dialogue," which he presented in his book *A Public Peace Process: Sustained Dialogue to Transform Racial and Ethnic Conflicts* (1999). In 2002, Saunders founded the Institute for Sustained Dialogue. Sustained dialogue encourages participants to converse with each other over a long period, recognizing the human dimension of their discussions, engaging as human beings who each carries their own pain and can learn to see others' pain, and beginning each meeting where the previous meeting left off. Saunders facilitated a sustained US–Russian dialogue as a successor of the Dartmouth Conference US–Soviet dialogue.

Sustained dialogues seek to develop compassion over time. By meeting over a long period, the participants develop a human connection with each other as individuals. The participants also develop a deep understanding for the concerns of the other participants that comes from conversations in both the formal sustained dialogue sessions and through meals and coffee breaks, where conversation is intense in small groups or in one-on-one interactions. Sustained dialogue's emphasis on recognizing the pain and concerns of each participant rests on the norms of compassion.

TRAINING AND DIALOGUE

Training programs can provide valuable forms of conflict resolution practice. While participants with various perspectives on a conflict situation are trained together in conflict resolution skills and techniques and exposed to examples of other conflicts, they can engage in dialogue regarding their own conflict. As Ronald Fisher (1997) writes, "training in conflict analysis and resolution can be seen as a form of interactive conflict resolution when it brings together members of conflicting groups to share a common learning experience that is based in part on the conflict between two sides" (335). As Fisher notes, these trainings have goals regarding the general skills and increased understandings of each other's perspectives on the conflict and possibilities for peacemaking in that specific conflict. However, to be appropriate as a form of interactive conflict resolution, training must be designed with consideration of cultural appropriateness and a balance of prescriptive, elicited, and interactive approaches (Fisher 1997).

The Burundi Leadership Training Program (BLTP) is an example of training as a form of interactive conflict resolution. It was developed by Howard Wolpe at the Woodrow Wilson International Center for Scholars, funded primarily by the World Bank, and designed "to increase the ability of the country's ethnically polarized leadership to work together" (Campbell and Uvin 2015, 281). The core of the dialogue centered around three six-day workshops held in Ngozi, where influential leaders from across the political spectrum in Burundi gathered to learn negotiation skills, build relationships, and engage in group problem-solving and strategic planning. With additional shorter follow-up workshops held to build on these longer foundational workshops, the dialogue process contributed to shifts in attitudes by participants and the development of improved relationships (Campbell and Uvin 2015). For several years after the August 2000 Arusha Peace and Reconciliation Agreement, the BLTP was influential in shaping more collaborative approaches during the transitional administration. But over time, as new political leadership became established in Burundi, the BLTP became a local Burundian NGO focused on training.

The BLTP's emphasis on developing improved understanding and fostering positive relationships required the development of compassion among the participants. As participants went through negotiation trainings and engaged in discussions on the future of Burundi together, they learned the perspectives and concerns of others. These understandings of the perspectives and concerns of others developed into compassion for all involved. As they developed compassion for each other, their attitudes shifted, and their relationships improved. The compassion developed through the BLTP allowed participants to encourage collaborative approaches during Burundi's transitional administration.

Moving Forward

At its core, the Rondine Method seeks to induce compassion among the students, which in turn rests on seeing their adversaries as complex beings, with their hardships, suffering, and pain that is worthy of sympathy. In humanizing the Other, such a method calls for recognizing the humanity in us all. To be sure, Rondine is not the peace education program that fosters compassion. For example, the youth peacebuilding and leadership program (YPLP), located in Brattleboro, Vermont, USA, brings youth together from conflict zones to engage in a one- or two-week training designed to foster relationship-building. The training consists of a series of dialogue sessions in which the students engage with their "enemy" counterparts (Ungerleider 2012).

But we are not aware of any research study regarding the inducement of compassion among the students of YPLP. In contrast, such a study has been launched for the Rondine program. In the spirit of its mission as a laboratory of peace, one author of this chapter (DR) implemented a research study in 2018 to determine whether Rondine students have in fact enhanced their sense of compassion. A cohort of fifteen students who entered Rondine in 2018 serve as subjects of three rounds of interviews, which occurred upon their entry in 2018, after one year of education/training in 2019, and upon their completion in 2020. This research study reflects an integration of peace education methods and social psychological measures for compassion. The preliminary results suggest that Rondine can serve as a model for fostering compassion as a critical element of peacebuilding globally. We plan to disseminate findings to peacebuilding scholar–practitioners.

Note

1. We thank the editors of *Conflict Resolution Quarterly* for permission to adapt our article "Building Peace through Systemic Compassion" (Rothbart and Allen 2019).

Conclusion

TODAY RONDINE, TOMORROW THE WORLD

Charles Hauss

In January 2019, my colleagues at the Alliance for Peacebuilding (AfP) asked me to represent the organization at an event organized by Rondine Cittadella della Pace at the Italian embassy in Washington. Even though I had been an exchange student in Italy and, therefore, spoke some Italian and had done research on the new left there early in my political science career, I had never heard of Rondine. So I spent the week before the event reading about its work and brushing up on my very rusty Italian. Still, it is safe to say that I had no idea that my life was about to change when I walked up Massachusetts Avenue to the embassy that morning.

I've spent more than fifty years as a professional peacebuilder and political scientist. During that time, I've worked with thousands of political science and conflict resolution students. So I was more than a little (and delightfully) surprised by how innovative the World House and Rondine's other projects seemed to be. Even more importantly, I was blown away by the current students and alumni I met who provided living proof that the Rondine Method worked.

I was scheduled to be on the final panel discussion of the afternoon, which was to be led by Miguel Díaz, whom I had never heard of before either. By the end of lunch, I had thrown my planned remarks into my iPad's trash bin and decided to just follow my instincts and react emotionally, as well as intellectually, to what I had seen and heard.

I honestly don't remember what I said, but it must have had an impact. A few weeks later, Franco Vaccari and his team invited me to visit Rondine and participate in a presentation they would be making to the Italian Senate in July. I was so taken by what my wife (also a senior fellow at AfP) saw that I found a way to include Rondine in the body of the introductory peacebuilding textbook that I was finishing for Rowman & Littlefield. My editor was so impressed that she suggested putting a picture of the village on the cover. I, of course, agreed (Hauss 2019).

Vaccari led a team from Rondine on another visit to the United States at the end of the year. While they were in Washington, they got to meet the staff of the Mary Hoch Center for Reconciliation (now the Think Peace Learning Hub), and they also got to see what Rondine was all about firsthand.

After they returned home, Vaccari got in touch with Miguel and me about the possibility of a book that combined a long essay on the Rondine Method, with some of the research being done about it that had been presented in the daylong event at the embassy. We eagerly agreed. Miguel decided to write the introduction, and I was asked to write a conclusion in which I explored what the Rondine Method might mean for the rest of us in the peacebuilding community.

That's what I plan to in this final chapter with its intentionally enigmatic title. In it, I will be taking you on a two-part journey that reflects my brief history with Rondine and its implications.

Hence, today Rondine, tomorrow the world.

Rondine Today

By the time I left the Italian embassy that afternoon, I knew I had to learn more about Rondine. It was already obvious that it had a lot to offer all of us who work on trauma healing, reconciliation, and more, which forced me to take a two-part essay on reconciliation that I was writing for Beyond Intractability back to the clichéd drawing board (Hauss 2021a, 2021b).

As I wrote those articles and began thinking about this one, I realized that two of the things about Rondine that have surfaced throughout this book should be singled out as its key contributions to the way we all go about dealing with intractable conflicts in general, and not just the ones that have brought students to Rondine for the last twenty years.

IT IS COMPREHENSIVE

First, it is safe to say that Rondine stands out because its program is so comprehensive. Other programs also cover much of the intellectual and political ground, and the Corrymeela Community and Rose Castle Foundation may even dig a bit more deeply into reconciliation per se.

However, the anecdotal evidence suggests that Rondine's work is more comprehensive in at least three ways. First, as you saw in Vaccari's chapters, Rondine gives young people time and space to confront emotional wounds that have built up over decades if not centuries. It is no accident that Vaccari himself is a trained clinical psychologist who incorporates what he has learned from decades of practice into the Rondine Method, something that cannot be said for most of my other colleagues who have designed and/or run reconciliation projects.

It might not be necessary for these kinds of programs to be run by mental health professionals. However, as the stepfather of a clinical psychologist and a longtime "consumer" of psychotherapy myself, I am convinced that people who are trained professionals should be at the heart of projects that deal with trauma healing, PTSD, and the like whenever possible.

As you saw in part 1, the young people who come to Rondine go through what amounts to two years of individual and group therapy. That part of the program goes beyond what they might get working with a conventional psychologist only in the sense that the individual and group work is all anchored in the conflicts that brought them to Rondine in the first place.

Although I've never heard anyone on the Rondine staff use this phrase, they orient the therapeutic part of their work around a question that is now commonplace in American communities that are dealing with the psychosocial impact of injustice.

What happened to you?

At first glance, that might not seem all that different from the questions you would be asked in a traditional intake session with a mental health professional. But subtly, it suggests that it is the traumatic event—the relational shock in Vaccari's term—that's the problem, not the patient's personal shortcomings.

Second, it is hard not to be impressed by the fact that Rondine incorporates academic studies into its practical work. Rondine is unique in that its students also leave with a master's degree from a local university. Not all students do the academic part of their stay in peace and conflict studies. Whatever the academic field they pursue, they all return home with a set of professional, as well as political, skills that they almost certainly could not have gotten at home.

Finally, the practical and academic work all have a leadership training component. It is not an accident that Rondine students are between the ages of twenty-one and thirty. Older individuals might know more about the conflicts or have more experience addressing them. However, Rondine's team is looking to identify young men and women who have the potential to lead their country's efforts in dealing with the conflict for the decades that it will take to make a serious dent in the structural and historical problems that produced the violence in the first place.

You can see that in two key features of the curriculum, which I thought Vaccari could have given more space to in part 1. First is the fact that the students are brought in pairs from both sides of their home country's conflict, and literally from the moment they arrive, they work on solving it *together*. Second and less obvious to me before I visited Rondine, you can't underestimate the importance of the fact that the second-year students mentor the newcomers as part of their own development. In other words, even before they go back home and launch their projects, the students have some practical experience as peace-building leaders who are implementing the Rondine Method.

BUT IT TAKES TIME

The second conclusion starts with a truism one finds in everything I've ever read about reconciliation and trauma healing. As I know from my own experience dealing with far less damaging emotional injuries than those suffered by the students at Rondine, you can't overcome the psychological scars left by intense conflict at a weekend retreat or through any other kind of short-term interven-tion. In fact, the professionals at Rondine understand that the students who have the luxury of spending two years in their village will spend a lifetime dealing with the personal costs of the PTSD, physical injuries, and other damages they have suffered.

Although everyone acknowledges the fact that reconciliation does not and cannot happen overnight, very few practitioners have found ways of enabling people who take part in peacebuilding processes to have the kind of time and training that Rondine offers. That's why the fact that the core Rondine program takes two years to complete is so important. In addition, we should not discount the fact that the students live together for that entire time and together chart the projects that they will undertake when they return.

Quite frankly, none of the other programs I know of come close to match-ing what Rondine offers its students in this respect. The Corrymeela Commu-nity (www.corrymeela.org), for instance, started out by providing a place for Catholics and Protestants to meet in Northern Ireland for prayer, reflection, and more even before the Troubles began in the late 1960s. It has grown into a community whose impact extends far beyond Northern Ireland and provides training and other services to peacebuilders from around the world. But it can-not expect the people of all ages who take part in its programs to undergo the kind of personal transformations we see at Rondine because they cannot spend two years in residence.

The same is true of the newer Rose Castle Foundation (www.rosecastlefoun-dation.org/). Architecturally, it comes closer than Rondine does to what most Americans have in mind when they think of a castle because it could easily have been used as the backdrop for a BBC series like *Downton Abbey*. Indeed, it had been the seat of the Anglican Bishop of Carlisle for centuries until it was sold to the Rose Castle Foundation for about $4 million in 2015. At that price, the Foundation had to be more than a reconciliation center. Indeed, your company can rent it as a site for a corporate retreat, or you can hold your wedding there. The purchasers want to use the proceeds they get from those rentals and their own endowment to fund Rose Castle's reconciliation efforts. Nonetheless, none of its founders have had the luxury of even thinking about creating a residential program that lasts for two years.

Academic programs like the one I'm associated with at George Mason University's (GMU's) Carter School of Peace and Conflict Resolution allow students to explore the theories underlying reconciliation in more depth than Rondine can. However, none of them brings together a cohort of twenty students a year, all of whom have both a lived experience with intractable conflict and an explicit commitment to exploring reconciliation as an alternative to the trauma they have lived through.

I raised GMU here not because Daniel Rothbart and Susan Allen are on its faculty and I have a courtesy research appointment there. In 2019, it became home to the Mary Hoch Center for Reconciliation and the related Think Peace project. While we have developed projects to provide psychological and social support to what we call insider reconcilers in places as different as the Horn of Africa, Finland, and a number of American cities, we cannot hope to provide the kind of intense and protracted engagement that Rondine offers.

Tomorrow the World

Now, to the hard part of this chapter as encapsulated in the second half of its title. Because you have gotten this far in the book, I assume that you share my enthusiasm for the Rondine Method.

However, I also assume that you at least thought about some the method's shortcomings, three of which are worth mentioning because they also point to the next steps that the Rondine community and people who share its goals could take. In fact, the Rondine team is well aware of them. They are justifiably proud of what they have accomplished over the last twenty years. Still, they understand that their tiny village in Tuscany cannot forge world peace or friendship among former enemies on its own. And as Vaccari implied at several points in his five chapters, the Rondine staff has taken steps to expand its impact in ways that go beyond what a program that can enroll only twenty students at a time can accomplish.

SCALING

I spend a lot of my time working with people whose peacebuilding and other forms of social change work were inspired by Silicon Valley start-ups. As a result, they spend a lot of time worrying about how best to take their initiatives to scale.

None of them think in terms of going to scale the way that Silicon Valley "unicorns" have by producing exponential growth that returns anything from a ten to one hundred times return on investment. While they may not want to become the peacebuilding equivalent of the so-called FANG companies (Facebook, Amazon, Netflix, and Google), they all want to grow exponentially in the three ways outlined in figure 10.1.

First, they want to scale "upward" so that they can have an impact on public policymaking. Second, they plan to scale "outward" and expand their impact on an ever-growing portion of the world's population. Finally, as Rondine shows us so clearly, we have to go to scale inward and develop more of the self-awareness that can take us toward being more empathetic, compassionate, and engaged.

As you saw in Vaccari's chapters, Rondine has taken steps in each of these directions. Obviously, "inner work" is at the heart of the two years the students spend there. In addition, the high school program for Italian *liceo* students and the young ambassadors for peace project, which drew me into Rondine's orbit, are evidence that it hopes to expand its impact outward and upward as well.

Still, when all is said and done, we cannot expect Rondine to play a leading role in taking its brand of peacebuilding work to scale. Its core program does take two years, which is more time than most future peacebuilders can afford to devote to any one program. What's more, Rondine is a very expensive program. It was given the village now known as Rondine by the local archbishop after all of its inhabitants had moved away. To be sure, it took a lot of sweat equity to turn the hamlet into the stunning village it is today. Nonetheless, it is hard to imagine any other NGO or university getting that kind of resource base to start

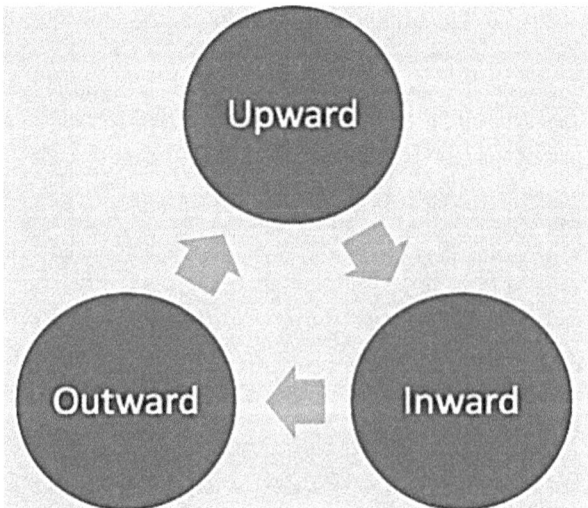

Figure 11.1

its work with. Last but by no means least, the program costs as much to maintain as any American graduate program that I'm aware of. It is hard, again, to imagine how any American (or other) graduate program could conceivably fund all of the travel, tuition, and living expenses of every one of its students.

TRANSLATING THE PRINCIPLES

That doesn't mean that Rondine's work cannot be taken to scale. As noted earlier, it can do some of that itself. More importantly, it can happen by others who can translate its concepts so that they can be added to work that they are already doing. Here, I don't mean literally translating its ideas into English, although that is no mean feat, as we discovered when we tried to convert Vaccari's Italian prose into an English that peacebuilders and other readers could relate to!

Rather, I am thinking more about what could be called a metaphoric translation through which practitioners and scholars adopt and then adapt some of the key concepts he raises in part 1 of this book and in everything else he has written over the years. And although Rondine's work contributes to all three ways organizations need to scale, its strength is clearly in the scaling inward portion of the triad.

If you will, Rondine and its method have hit the peacebuilding and social change communities writ large at a time when more and more of my colleagues are coming to grips with the need to stress inner work. In that respect, Rondine's arrival in the English-speaking world could not have come at a more auspicious moment. That holds, in particular, for those of us who stress the importance of locally led peacebuilding and/or the need for a cultural paradigm shift in the ways we deal with each other as the other scholar–practitioners who contributed chapters for part 2 of this volume have put it in their specific ways.

More generally, it us up to practitioners and activists like me (and I suspect that will include most readers of this book) to take the method's key concepts and use them in ways that make sense in the contexts in which they work. Some of those concepts will be familiar to many of us, including the image of the enemy and the ways we stereotype the Other, which you can see, for instance, in all of the references to contact theory in part 2.

Others, however, are quite new. For example, I'm drawn to Vaccari's idea of a relational shock and his reliance on some of the architects of modern and postmodern social psychology and related disciplines such as Donald Winnicott, Simone Weil, Martin Buber, Edgar Morin, and others. Although I had read works by most of them before, I had not seen all of the ways in which their work is relevant to the kind of peacebuilding my colleagues at the AfP do around the world. Here, I find Vaccari's notion of the sudden ways that what he calls relational shocks can make effective and constructive relationship between people on either side of an intractable conflict all but impossible.

SO WE CAN MEET SOME COUSINS WE DIDN'T KNOW WE HAD (OR NEEDED)

On the assumption, again, that Rondine can't "do it all," let me end this section with perhaps its most important point. We need to incorporate as much of the Rondine Method as we can in the work that the rest of us do. That holds, first of all, for my fellow peacebuilders. If anything, learning those lessons could prove to be even more important for colleagues who work for social change in other arenas.

There are peacebuilders whose work overlaps with Rondine's. Chad Ford, for example, has built his career using basketball as a jumping off point through Peace Players International. More germane here is his recent book, *Dangerous Love* (Ford 2020), in which he stresses the importance of taking first steps and turning toward the people we disagree with.

I suspect, however, that Rondine will have an even greater impact on individuals and organizations that do not put peacebuilding per se on center stage.

Thus, Ford works closely with the Arbinger Institute, which can best be described as a consulting firm that helps corporate, NGO, and governmental clients shift toward what it calls an outward mindset (Arbinger 2022). Arbinger uses different terminology, focusing on the costs of what it calls an "inward mind set." Still, the overlap between its work and Rondine's is considerable—despite the fact that Arbinger workshops are not held with a Tuscan backdrop.

If I'm right, however, Rondine can have an even greater impact once its ideas can be shared with intellectual "cousins" who rarely think in terms of peacebuilding or conflict resolution per se. I am an early investor in Zebras Unite Co-op (www.zebrasunite.coop), which describes itself as a "founder-led, cooperatively owned global movement creating the culture, capital & community for the next economy." In the two years I've worked with the Zebras and its dazzle (yes, zebras do come together in dazzles rather than herds), I've seen it coming to grips with many of the same issues that the Rondine students grapple with, but in this case the challenge is rebuilding capitalism rather than overcoming political divisions.

It's not just unconventional organizations like the Zebras that refer to their founders as doulas who are giving birth to the next economy. You find limited versions of the method being taught in America's top MBA programs by faculty members who have never heard of Rondine. Thus, Robert Sutton (2007) focuses on what he calls the "no asshole rule" as the key to successful management. Amy Edmondson (2018) has become one of Harvard Business School's most famous and beloved professors because of her work in understanding what she calls "fearless organizations." Adam Grant (2013) burst onto the scene as part of the next generation of organizational leaders with his book *Give and Take*, which explores how and why more and more leaders succeed because they put "giving" to others ahead of "taking" as much as they can for themselves.

In the end, I'll forever be grateful to my three colleagues at AfP who could not make the meeting in Rondine held at the Italian embassy that day in 2019. Because I ended up being the AfP representative at the symposium, I found the Rondine Method, which is now at the heart of everything I do in my efforts to change American cultural norms and public policy as we navigate our way through this century's version of the Roaring Twenties.

From Chechnya to Ukraine: Why We Need Rondines (in the Plural)

As you also saw in part 1, Rondine got its start when Vaccari invited Russian and Chechen young people to come live together in the village, which he and his colleagues were in the process of rebuilding. Ironically, this book went to press during the eleventh month of Russia's brutal invasion of Ukraine. It was therefore hard not to be struck by the parallels with Russia's wars with Chechnya, which played such a pivotal role in Rondine's creation.

This is not the place to discuss the geopolitics and morality (or lack thereof) behind the conflict. Instead, I want to end this book by pointing out two parallels between the conflicts that drive home the point I have been making in this concluding chapter.

They both clearly demonstrate the importance of what Rondine does. Vaccari and his colleagues already see the need of inviting young Russians and Ukrainians to spend two years at the World House. In some ways, having them there will be easier than has been the case with the other conflicts Rondine has addressed because Russians and Ukrainians can readily understand each other's languages and because so many of their families have intermarried over the years. At the same time, it is likely to be harder for them to understand each other in the ways that Vaccari talks about in part 2 precisely because they have all of those superficial similarities that have been shattered by a war that has been every bit as brutal as the two Russia fought with Chechen separatists at the end of the twentieth century and the beginning of this one.

At the same time, it is also clear that Rondine cannot do that work alone. All of us will have to do our part in our own ways—ways that could and should be informed by the ideas we have talked about in this book.

That is why we need Rondines (in the plural).

Bibliography

Adelmann, Bob. 2012. "Two Years After Haiti's Earthquake, Where Did the Money Go?" January 17, 2012. *New American.* https://thenewamerican.com/two-years-after-haiti-earthquake-where-did-the-money-go/.

Alici, Luca. 2018. *Fidarsi. All'origine del legame sociale.* Trieste: Meudon.

Alici, Luca, ed. 2019. *Dentro il conflitto, oltre il nemico. Il "Metodo Rondine."* Bologna: Editrice il Mulino.

Allen, Susan H. 2015. "Estonia: Psychopolitical Dialogue Contributing to Conflict Prevention." In *Across the Lines of Conflict*, edited by M. Lund and S. McDonald, 53–84. Washington, DC: Woodrow Wilson Center Press.

Allen, Susan. 2018. "Consciousness and Rondine." In *Metodo Rondine: trasformazione creativa dei conflitti*, edited by Franco Vaccari, 329–33. Villa Verucchio: Pazzini edizione bilingue.

Allport, G. W. 1954. *The Nature of Prejudice.* Reading, MA: Addison-Wesley.

Al Ramiah, Ananthi, and Miles Hewstone. 2013. "Intergroup Contact as a Tool for Reducing, Resolving, and Preventing Intergroup Conflict: Evidence, Limitations, and Potential." *American Psychologist* 68, no. 7: 527–42.

Antonovsky, A. 1987. *Unraveling the Mystery of Health: How People Manage Stress and Stay Well.* San Francisco, CA: Jossey-Bass.

Appleby, R. Scott, and Richard Cizik. 2015. "Engaging Religious Communities Abroad: A New Imperative for U.S. Foreign Policy." *Report of the Task Force on Religion and the Making of U.S. Foreign Policy.* Accessed May 1, 2022, https://keough.nd.edu/wp-content/uploads/2015/12/engaging_religious_communities_abroad.pdf.

Arbinger Institute. 2022. *The Anatomy of Conflict: Resolving the Heart of Peace.* 4th ed. San Francisco: Berrett-Koehler.

Aron, A., E. N. Aron, and D. Smollan. 1992. "Inclusion of Other in the Self Scale and the Structure of Interpersonal Closeness." *Journal of Personality and Social Psychology* 63: 596–612.

Assagioli, Roberto. 2018. *Che cos'è la Psicosintesi*. consultazione del 31 luglio 2019. www .psicosintesi.it.

Bamat, Tom, Nell Bolton, Myla Leguro, and Atalia Omer, eds. 2017. *Interreligious Action for Peace: Studies in Muslim-Christian Cooperation*. Catholic Relief Services. Accessed May 2, 2022. https://www.crs.org/our-work-overseas/research-publications /interreligious-action-peace.

Banchoff, Thomas. 2008. "The Circle of Dialogue." In *Islam and the West: Annual Report on the State of Dialogue*, edited by N. Tranchet and D. Rienstra. Geneva: World Economic Forum.

Bar-Tal, D. 2013. *Intractable Conflicts: Socio-Psychological Foundations and Dynamics*. New York, NY: Cambridge University Press.

Bar-Tal, D., K. Sharvit, E. Halperin, and A. Zafran. 2012. "Ethos of Conflict: The Concept and Its Measurement." *Peace and Conflict: Journal of Peace Psychology* 18: 40–61.

Bateson, Gregory. 2000. *Steps to an Ecology of Mind*. Chicago, IL: University of Chicago Press.

BBC. 2009. "Russia Vows to Protect S Ossetia." Modified August 26, 2009. Accessed November 18, 2011. http://news.bbc.co.uk/2/hi/8223443.stm.

Benasayag, Miguel, and Angélique del Rey. 2008. *Elogio del conflitto*. Milano: Feltrinelli.

Benjamin, Jessica. 2017. *Beyond Doer and Done To: Recognition Theory, Intersubjectivity and the Third*. London: Routledge.

Berents, Helen. 2015. "An Embodied Everyday Peace in the Midst of Violence." *Peacebuilding* 3, no. 2: 1–14.

Bertoni, A., M. Parise, and R. Iafrate. 2012. "Beyond Satisfaction: Generativity as a New Outcome of Couple Functioning." In *Marriage: Psychological Implications, Social Expectations, and Role of Sexuality*, edited by P. E. Esposito and C. I. Lombardi, 115–32. Hauppauge, NY: Nova Science.

Beyleveld, D., and R. Brownsword. 1998. "Human Dignity, Human Rights, and Human Genetics." *Modern Law Review* 61: 661–80.

Bierhoff, Hans W., Renate Klein, and Peter Kamp. 1991. "Evidence for the Altruistic Personality from Data on Accident Research." *Journal of Personality* 59: 263–80.

Bin Muhammad, Ghazi, and Melissa Yarrington, eds. 2010. *A Common Word: Muslims and Christians on Loving God and Neighbor*. Grand Rapids, MI: William B. Eerdmans.

Bourdieu, P. 1977. *Outline of a Theory of Practice*. Cambridge, UK: Cambridge University Press.

Brewer, M. B., and N. Miller. 1984. *Groups in Contact: The Psychology of Desegregation*. New York, NY: Academic Press.

Buber, Martin. 1937. *I and Thou*. Edinburgh: T. and T. Clark.

Burton, J. W. 1969. *Conflict and Communication: The Use of Controlled Communication in International Relations*. London: Macmillan.

Bush, R., and J. Folger. 2005. *The Promise of Mediation: The Transformative Approach to Conflict*. San Francisco, CA: Jossey-Bass.

Caillé, Alain. 1998. *Di chi fidarsi? Dono, fiducia e indebitamento reciproco*. Appears as an appendix in Jacques Godbout. 1998. *Il linguaggio del dono*. Torino: Bollati Boringhieri.

Campbell, S., and P. Uvin 2015. "The Burundi Leadership Training Program." In *Across the Lines of Conflict*, edited by M. Lund and S. McDonald, 281–312. Washington, DC: Woodrow Wilson Center Press.

Capozza, D., E. Trifiletti, L. Vezzali, and E. Favara. 2013. "Can Intergroup Contact Improve Humanity Attributions?" *International Journal of Psychology* 48, no. 4: 527–41.

Chigas, Diana. 2015. "The Harvard Study Group on Cyprus: Contributions to an Unfulfilled Peace Process." In *Across the Lines of Conflict: Facilitating Cooperation to Build Peace*, edited by Michael Lund and Steve McDonald, 231–80. New York, NY: Columbia University Press.

Corbella, Silvia. 2005. "Presentazione a Panizza, Sandro 2012." *Per una psicoanalisi bipersonale*. Milano: Franco Angeli.

Corrao, S. 2000. *Il focus group*. Milano: Franco Angeli.

Díaz, Miguel H. 2018. "Preface." In *Metodo Rondine: trasformazione creativa dei conflitti*, Franco Vaccari. Villa Verucchio: Pazzini edizione bilingue.

_____. 2019. *Young Leaders for Peace Teach Us to Make Room for Difference*. National Catholic Reporter. Posted April 9, 2019. https://www.ncronline.org/opinion/theology -en-la-plaza/young-leaders-peace-teach-us-make-room-difference.

Dicke, K. 2002. "The Founding Function of Human Dignity in the Universal Declaration of Human Rights." In *The Concept of Human Dignity in Human Rights Discourse*, edited by D. Kretzmer and E. Klein, 111–20. New York, NY: Kluwer Law International.

Donnelly, J. 1982. "Human Rights and Human Dignity: An Analytic Critique of Non-Western Conceptions of Human Rights." *American Political Science Review* 76: 303–16.

Edmondson, Amy. 2018. *The Fearless Organization: Creating Psychological Safety in the Workplace for Learning, Innovation, and Growth*. New York, NY: Wiley.

Elliott, Justin, and Laura Sullivan. 2015. "How the Red Cross Raised Half a Billion Dollars for Haiti and Built Six Homes." ProPublica. Published June 3, 2015. https:// www.propublica.org/article/how-the-red-cross-raised-half-a-billion-dollars-for-haiti -and-built-6-homes.

Engle Merry, Sally. 2007. "Part III: Conditions of Vulnerability: Introduction." In *The Practice of Human Rights: Tracking Law between the Global and the Local*, edited by Mark Goodale and Sally Engle Merry, 195–203. Cambridge, UK: Cambridge University Press.

Erikson, Erik. 1950. *Childhood and Society*. New York, NY: W.W. Norton.

Fisher, Ronald. J. 1997. *Interactive Conflict Resolution*. Syracuse, NY: Syracuse University Press.

Fogelman, E. 1994. *Conscience and Courage: Rescuers of Jews during the Holocaust*. New York, NY: Doubleday.

Ford, Chad. 2020. *Dangerous Love: Transforming Fear and Conflict at Home, at Work, and in the World*. San Francisco, CA: Berrett-Koehler.

Frankl, Viktor. 1962. *Man's Search for Meaning*. Boston, MA: Beacon Press.

Fredrickson, B. L., M. A. Cohn, K. A. Coffey, J. Pek, and S. M. Finkel. 2008. "Open Hearts Build Lives: Positive Emotions, Induced through Lovingkindness Meditation,

Build Consequential Personal Resources." *Journal of Personality and Social Psychology* 95: 1045–62.

Fulmer, R. H. 1983. "Teaching the Family Life Space: A Guide for a Workshop Using Simulated Families." *American Journal of Family Therapy* 11: 55–63.

Galantino, Nunzio. 2018. *Abitare le parole. Per un vocabolario dell'esistenza*, con prefazione di papa Francesco. Milano: Piemme-Mondadori.

Galimberti, Umberto. 1992. *Dizionario di psicologia*. Torino: Utet.

Galston, W. A. 1993. "Cosmopolitan Altruism." *Social Philosophy and Social Policy* 10: 118–34.

Galtung, Johan. 2004. *Transcend and Transform: An Introduction to Conflict Work*. London: Pluto Press.

Godbout, Jacques. 1998. *Il linguaggio del dono*. Torino: Bollati Boringhieri.

Goizueta, Roberto S. 1995. *Caminemos Con Jesús: Toward a Hispanic/Latino Theology of Accompaniment*. Maryknoll, NY: Orbis Books.

Goldstein, S. B. 1999. "Construction and Validation of a Conflict Communication Scale." *Journal of Applied Social Psychology* 29: 1803–32.

Gopin, Marc. 2000. *Between Eden and Armageddon: The Future of World Religions, Violence, and Peacemaking*. Oxford: Oxford University Press.

Grant, Adam. 2013. *Give and Take: Why Helping Others Drives Our Success*. New York, NY: Viking.

Hauss, Charles. 2019. *From Conflict Resolution to Peacebuiliding*. Lanham, MD: Rowman & Littlefield.

———— 2021a. "Reconciliation Part 1: What Is Reconciliation? https://www.beyondintractability.org/essay/reconciliation.

———— 2021b. "Reconciliation Part 2: Making Reconciliation Happen." https://www.beyondintractability.org/essay/reconciliation-part2.

Henckaerts, Jean-Marie, and Louis Doswald-Beck. 2005. *Practice*. Volume II of *Customary International Humanitarian Law*. Cambridge, UK: Cambridge University Press.

Hewstone, M., and R. Brown. 1986. "Contact Is Not Enough: An Intergroup Perspective on the 'Contact Hypothesis.'" In *Contact and Conflict in Intergroup Encounters*, edited by M. Hewstone and R. Brown, 1–44. New York, NY: Basil Blackwell.

Iafrate, R., and A. Bertoni. 2019. "Rondine Cittadella della Pace: un laboratorio a cielo aperto sul conflitto intergruppi e sull'ipotesi del contatto." In *Dietro il conflitto, oltre il nemico il "Metodo Rondine,"* edited by L. Alici, 115–30. Bologna, Italy: Il Mulino.

Illich, Ivan. 2009. "L'impresa educativa attuale vista con gli occhi dell'emarginato." In *La perdita dei sensi*. Firenze: Libreria Editrice Fiorentina.

Johnston, Laurie. 2008. "'To Be Holy in the World': The Influence of Yves Congar on the Spirituality and Practice of the Community of Sant'Egidio." *Catholic Identity and the Laity: The Annual Publication of the College Theology Society*, edited by Tim Muldoon, 59–74. Maryknoll, NY: Orbis Books.

Jung, Carl Gustav. (1916) 2003. *The Psychology of the Unconscious*. New York, NY: Dover.

————. 1967. *Symbols of Transformation*. Princeton, NJ: Princeton University Press.

Keith, Morgan. 2021. "The American Red Cross' Performance in Haiti Has Become the Focus of Critics Who Urge People Not to Donate to the Organization." Yahoo.com. Published August 31, 2021. https://www.yahoo.com/news/american-red-cross-2010 -performance-231146133.html.

Kelman, H. 1972. "The Problem-Solving Workshop in Conflict Resolution." In *Communication in International Politics*, edited by R. L. Merritt, 168–204. Champaign, IL: University of Illinois Press.

Klimecki, O. 2015. "The Plasticity of Social Emotions." *Social Neuroscience* 10, no. 5: 466–73.

Klimecki, O., S. Leiberg, M. Ricard, and T. Singer. 2014. "Differential Pattern of Functional Brain Plasticity after Compassion and Empathy Training." *Social, Cognitive and Affect Neuroscience* 9: 873–79.

Krebs, Dennis L., and Frank Van Hesteren. 1992. "The Development of Altruistic Personality." In *Embracing the Other: Philosophical, Psychological, and Historical Perspectives on Altruism*, edited by Pearl M. Oliner, Samuel P. Oliner, Lawrence Baron, Lawrence A. Blum, Dennis Krebs, and M. Zuzanna Smoleneska, 142–69. New York, NY: New York University Press.

Lederach, John Paul, Reina Neufeldt, and Hal Culbertson. 2007. *Reflective Peacebuilding: A Planning, Monitoring, and Learning Tool Kit*. Notre Dame, IN: Joan B. Kroc Institute for International Peace Studies, University of Notre Dame.

Leone, L., and Prezza, M. 1999. *Costruire e valutare i progetti nel sociale. Manuale operativo per chi lavora su progetti in campo sanitario, sociale, educativo e culturale*. Milano: Franco Angeli.

Levinas, Emmanuel. 1983. *Time and the Other*. New York, NY: Columbia University Press.

Lewin, K. 1946. "Action Research and Minority Problems." *Journal of Social Issues* 2: 34–46.

Lingiardi, Vittorio. 2019. *Io, tu, noi. Vivere con se stessi, l'altro, gli altri*. Milano: Utetlibri-DeA Planeta Libri.

Lutz, A., J. Brefczynski-Lewis, T. Johnstone, and R. Davidson. 2008. "Regulation of the Neutral Circuitry of Emotion by Compassion Meditation: Effects of Meditative Expertise." *PLOS One*, March 26. Accessed July 14, 2018. https://doi.org/10.1371/journal.pone.0001897.

Mac Ginty, R. 2014. "Everyday Peace, Bottom-Up and Local Agency in Conflict Affected Societies." *Security Dialogue* 456: 548–64.

Mac Ginty, R., and P. Firchow. 2016. "Top-Down and Bottom-Up Narratives of Peace and Conflict." *Politics* 363: 308–23.

McAdams, D. P., and E. de St. Aubin. 1992. "A Theory of Generativity and Its Assessment through Self-Report, Behavioral Acts, and Narrative Themes in Autobiography." *Journal of Personality and Social Psychology* 62: 1003–15.

McKeown, S., and L. K. Taylor. 2017. "Intergroup Contact and Peacebuilding: Promoting Youth Civic Engagement in Northern Ireland." *Journal of Social and Political Psychology* 5, no. 2.

Mitchell, C. R. 2005. *Resolving Intractable Conflicts: A Handbook*. London: Palgrave Macmillan.

Mitchell, C. R., and M. Banks. 1996. *Handbook of Conflict Resolution: The Analytical Problem-Solving Approach*. New York, NY: Continuum.

Morelli, Giovanna. 2017. "Ivan Illich e la fenomenologia dell'incarnazione." In *In cammino sullo spartiacque. Scritti su Ivan Illich*, edited by Adalberto Arrigoni, Emmanuele Morandi, and Riccardo Prandini. Milano-Udine: Mimesis.

_____. 2019. *Poetica dell'incarnazione. Prospettive mitobiografiche nell'analisi filosofica.* Milano-Udine: Mimesis.

Morin, Edgar. 1993. *Il Metodo.* Volume 4 in *Le idee: habitat, vita, organizzazione, usi e costumi.* Milano: Raffaello Cortina.

_____. 2008. *On Complexity.* New York, NY: Hampton Press.

Mounier, Emmanuel. 1986. *Personalism.* South Bend, IN: University of Notre Dame Press.

Nan, S. A., and J. Greiff. 2013. "Basic Human Needs in Practice: The Georgian-South Ossetian Point of View Process." In *Conflict Resolution and Human Needs: Linking Theory and Practice*, edited by K. Avruch and C. R. Mitchell, 202–15. New York, NY: Routledge.

Neufeldt, Reina. 2016. "Interfaith Dialogue: Assessing Theories of Change." *Peace and Change* 36, no. 3. For examples of how these theories are applied in a particular conflict, see Catholic Relief Services, Documentation, Inter-religious Dialogue Stakeholders Meeting, Mindanao Training Resource Center, Davao City, March 3–4.

Nussbaum, Martha. 2001. *Upheavals of Thought: The Intelligence of Emotions*. New York, NY: Cambridge University Press.

Oliner, P., and S. Oliner. 1988. *The Altruistic Personality: Rescuers of Jews in Nazi Europe.* New York, NY: Free Press.

Oliverio, Alberto. 2013. *Immaginazione e memoria. Fantasia e realtà nei processi mentali.* Milano: Mondadori Università.

Ozawa-de Silva, B., B. Dodson-Lavell, C. Raison, and L. Negi. 2012. "Compassion and Ethics: Scientific and Practical Approaches to the Cultivation of Compassion as a Foundation for Ethical Subjectivity and Well-Being." *Journal of Healthcare, Science and the Humanities* 21: 145–61.

Natoli, Salvatore. 2016. *Il rischio di fidarsi.* Bologna: Il Mulino.

Pagani, A. F., and A. Garuglieri. 2019. "Rondine Cittadella della Pace: una ricerca di valutazione." In *Dietro il conflitto, oltre il nemico il "Metodo Rondine,"* edited by L. Alici, 131–69. Bologna: Il Mulino.

Panizza, Sandro. 2005. *Per una psicoanalisi bipersonale.* Milano: Franco Angeli.

Pettigrew, T. F. 1998. "Intergroup Contact Theory." *Annual Review of Psychology* 49: 65–85.

Pope Francis. 2015. *Laudato Si': On Care for Our Common Home.* Vatican. Accessed May 1, 2022. https://www.vatican.va/content/francesco/en/encyclicals/documents/papa-francesco_20150524_enciclica-laudato-si.html.

_____. 2020. *Fratelli tutti.* Vatican. Accessed May 2, 2022. https://www.vatican .va/content/francesco/en/encyclicals/documents/papa-francesco_20201003_enciclica -fratelli-tutti.html.

Rastelli, Alessia. 2018. *Caro nemico, abbracciamoci.* Corriere della Sera, July 15, 2018.

Ricoeur, Paul. 1990. *Oneself as Another.* Chicago, IL: University of Chicago Press.

Rogers, E. S., J. Chamberlin, M. L. Ellison, and T. Crean. 1997. "A Consumer-Constructed Scale to Measure Empowerment among Users of Mental Health Services." *Psychiatric Services* 48: 1042–47.

Romany, C. 1994. "State Responsibility Goes Private." In *Human Rights of Women—National and International Perspectives*, edited by R. J. Cook, 85–115. Philadelphia, PA: University of Pennsylvania Press.

Rothbart, Daniel, and Susan Allen. 2019. "Building Peace through Systemic Compassion." *Conflict Resolution Quarterly* 36, no. 4: 373–86.

Rothbart, Daniel, and Jessica Cooley. 2016. "Hutus Aiding Tutsis during the Rwandan Genocide: Motives, Meanings and Morals." *Genocide Studies and Prevention: An International Journal* 10, no. 2: 76–97. http://dx.doi.org/10.5038/1911-9933.10.2.1398.

Rothbart, Daniel, and Karina Korostelina. 2006. "Moral Denigration of the Other." In *Identity, Morality, and Threat: Studies in Violent Conflict*, edited by D. Rothbart and K. Korostelina. Rowman & Littlefield.

Rye, M. S., D. M. Loiacono, C. D. Folck, B. T. Olszewski, T. A. Heim, and B. P. Madia. 2001. "Evaluation of the Psychometric Properties of Two Forgiveness Scales." *Current Psychology* 20: 260–77.

Saakashvili, M. 2008. "Saakashvili's Televised Address on S. Ossetia." Civil Georgia. Posted August 7, 2008. Accessed November 18, 2011. http://www.civil.ge/eng/article.php?id=18934.

Sacks, Jonathan. 2002. *The Dignity of Difference*. New York, NY: Continuum International Publishing.

Saunders, Harold. H. 1999. *A Public Peace Process: Sustained Dialogue to Transform Racial and Ethnic Conflicts*. New York, NY: Palgrave.

Schreiter, Robert J., R. Scott Appleby, and Gerard F. Powers. 2010. *Peacebuilding: Catholic Theology, Ethics, and Praxis*. Maryknoll, NY: Orbis Books.

Singer, T., and O. Klimecki. 2014. "Empathy and Compassion." *Current Biology* 2418: R875–78.

Sterling, P., and J. Eyer. 1988. "Allostasis: A New Paradigm to Explain Arousal Pathology." In *Handbook of Life Stress, Cognition, and Health*, edited by S. Fisher and J. T. Reason. Chicester, NY: Wiley.

Suedfeld, P., and S. de Best. 2008. "Value Hierarchies of Holocaust Rescuers and Resistance Fighters." *Genocide Studies and Prevention* 31: 38–40.

Sutton, Robert. 2007. *The No Asshole Rule: Building a Civilized Workplace and Surviving One That Isn't*. New York, NY: Business Plus.

Tajfel, H., and J. C. Turner. 1979. "An Integrative Theory of Inter-Group Conflict." In *The Social Psychology of Inter-Group Relations*, edited by W. G. Austin and S. Worchel, 33–47. Monterey, CA: Brooks/Cole.

Trevi, Mario. 1987. *Per uno junghismo critico*. Milano: Bompiani.

———. 2012. *Introduzione* a C.G. Jung 1928, *L'Io e l'inconscio*. Torino: Bollati Boringhieri.

Ungerleider, J. 2012. "Structured Youth Dialogue to Empower Peacebuilding and Leadership." *Conflict Resolution Quarterly* 29: 381–401.

———. 2018a. *Metodo Rondine: trasformazione creativa dei conflitti*. Villa Verucchio: Pazzini edizione bilingue.

_____ 2018b. *S-confinamenti. Un approccio al conflitto.* Villa Verucchio: Pazzini edizione bilingue.

_____ 2018c. *StoRYcycle. La bellezza di storie rovesciate.* Villa Verucchio: Pazzini edizione bilingue.

Vaccari, Franco, and Francesca Simeoni. 2019. *Rondine Cittadella della Pace. Storie di nemici che s'incontrano.* Cinisello Balsamo: Edizioni San Paolo.

Volkan, Vamic. 1997. *Blood Lines: From Ethnic Pride to Ethnic Terrorism.* Boulder, CO: Westview Press.

Wallace, Nichole, and Caroline Preston. 2011. "Haiti Earthquake: One Year Later. American Donors Gave $1.4-Billion to Haiti Aid." *The Chronicle of Philanthropy.* Published January 6, 2011. https://www.philanthropy.com/article/american-donors-gave-1-4-billion-to-haiti-aid/.

Ward, C., J. Stuart, and L. Kus. 2011. "The Construction and Validation of a Measure of Ethno-Cultural Identity Scale." *Journal of Personality Assessment* 93: 462–73.

Webster, Donovan. 2012. "Haiti Earthquake: Two Years Later, Where Did the Money Go?" Published January 12, 2012. Modified December 6, 2017. *HuffPost.* https://www.huffpost.com/entry/haiti-earthquake-funds_n_1200229.

Weil, Simone. 1950. *Waiting for God.* London: Routledge.

Wilkinson, I. 1987. "Family Assessment: A Review." *Journal of Family Therapy* 5: 367–80.

Winnicott, Donald Woods. 1971. *Playing and Reality.* London: Tavistock.

Index

Abkhaz, 115,116, 149
accompaniment, 4, 104, 142, 149
Africa, 23, 25, 133, 149
Allen, Susan, x, xii, 11, 12, 21, 25, 104,
    113,114, 116, 118, 120, 122, 124,
    126, 127, 133, 139, 145, 147, 149
Allport, Gordon, 80, 139, 149
Anthropology, 18–20, 31, 37, 149
appeal, xvi, 11, 17, 110, 149
Arendt, Hannah, 16, 149
Armenia, 30, 62, 86, 149
authenticity, 15, 28, 149
Azerbaijan, 14, 30, 60, 86, 149

Balkans, 23, 149
Bateson, Gregory, 71, 74, 140, 149
belonging, xvi, 15, 20, 28, 80, 81, 84,
    149
Binswanger, Ludwig, 40
bottom up, 98, 101, 149
bridge, xiii, 3, 7, 59, 61, 63, 65, 66, 73,
    102, 110, 149, 152
Buber, Martin, 38, 44, 68, 71, 135, 140,
    149

Caillé, Alain, 41, 140
Catholic, xi, 6,7, 13, 86, 100, 106, 140,
    142, 144, 145, 148, 149

celebration, 71, 149
Chechen, 16,17, 137, 149
collaboration, 5, 14, 18,54, 109, 121,
    12,126, 149
common good, xvi, xvii, 28, 109
common ground, 27, 46, 52, 103,
    107,110, 149
common humanity, 2, 4, 55, 81
community, vii, xvi, 2, 5, 6, 14, 17, 22,
    23, 28, 31, 71,73, 98,99, 101, 104,
    105, 108, 110, 120, 130, 132, 133,
    136, 142, 149, 151
compassion, x, 16, 49, 68, 104,105, 113,
    127, 143, 145, 149
comprehensive, 130
conflict, iii, vii, ix,x, xii,xiii, xv,xvi, 2,7,
    11,14, 16, 21, 25, 28,31, 34, 37,
    39,40, 42,43, 51, 56, 60, 61, 63, 65,
    67, 70, 72,73, 79, 81, 83, 84, 86,
    89, 93, 98, 100, 103, 111, 113,117,
    120,127, 129, 131,133, 136,137,
    139,145, 147, 149
conflict resolution, 6, 12, 36, 72, 103,
    106, 114,117, 121, 127, 129, 133,
    136, 141,145, 147,149
conflict transformation, x, xii, 37, 65, 67,
    103, 106, 149
confligere, 43

conscience, 16, 141, 149
consciousness, 12, 113, 123, 139, 149
contact theory, x, 6, 79, 81, 103, 105, 107, 111, 135, 144, 150
Corrymeela, 130, 132, 150
courage, xvii, 13, 59, 121, 141, 150
creativity, 37, 39, 41, 42, 49, 150
crisis, 19, 24, 27, 28, 30, 33, 53, 74, 102, 150
culture, xii, xv, 2, 4, 13, 14, 19, 20, 25, 31, 37, 41, 42, 46, 47, 49, 53, 88, 104, 106, 109, 126, 135–137, 146, 150
culture of coexistence, 106
culture of encounter, 104

deceptive switch, 57
deconstructing, 35, 59
defense, xvi, 11, 97,102, 150
delusional, 32, 33, 46, 150
development, xv, 19, 27, 39, 42, 61, 83, 97, 103, 114, 121, 124, 126, 132, 143, 150
dialogue, xvi, xvii, 2, 7, 11, 14, 18, 33, 37, 40, 42, 45, 47, 48, 52, 59, 62, 71, 72, 103, 104, 107, 110, 114, 116, 117, 121, 126, 139, 140, 143, 145, 150
different-concrete, 24, 27, 34, 150
dignity, xvi, 69, 105, 118, 119, 140, 141, 145, 150
diplomacy, 3, 7, 17, 97, 102, 116, 121, 122, 125, 150
distortion, 56, 57, 150
diversity, 20, 27, 29, 38, 69, 81, 150

empathy, 106, 114, 117, 118, 143, 145, 150
enemy, ix, xii, xv, xvii, 1, 3, 6, 12, 18, 21–25, 29, 30, 32, 34, 37, 43, 51, 53, 55, 58, 62–64 , 66, 68, 69, 74, 75, 81, 84, 85, 87, 89, 99, 103, 105, 110, 111, 126, 133, 135 150
enmity, 13, 61, 107, 113, 123, 150
Erikson, Erik, 19, 39, 40, 68, 141, 150

evaluation, 79, 81,85, 93, 145, 150
evolution, 28, 31, 52, 65, 71 150

face, 2, 3, 15, 28, 33, 38, 43, 45, 47, 56, 60, 64, 68, 80, 84, 100, 105, 108
facilitation, 21, 104, 150
fantasy, 24, 34, 41,42, 58, 150
foreign aid, 98, 100, 102, 150
foreign policy, x, 97, 99, 102, 139
fragile, 28, 55, 104, 150
fragility, 18, 55, 94, 150
Frankl, Victor, 65, 68, 141, 150
friend, xii, 17, 23, 150
friendship, 11, 18, 20, 24, 28, 104, 105, 109, 133, 150

Galtung, Johan, 55, 142, 150
Generations, xv ixvi, 14, 28, 69
genocide, 105, 114, 119, 121, 145, 150
George Mason University, 11, 116, 133, 147,148, 150
Georgia, 33, 86, 115, 145, 150
ghost, 33–35, 41, 61, 66, 69, 150
globalization, 21, 150
group, iv, 14,15, 21, 23, 34, 39, 54,55, 62, 71, 79, 80, 84, 87, 89, 95, 105, 107, 114, 116, 118, 120, 123, 124, 126, 131, 141, 145, 150, 151

Habitus, 72, 120, 151
Haiti, 99, 139, 141, 143, 146, 151
hallucination, 32, 34,35, 56, 151
hate, 15, 16, 32, 33, 60, 151
Hauss, Charles, 1, 3,17, 19, 59, 61, 63, 65, 81, 83, 104, 106, 108, 110, 134, 136,148, 151
holistic, 5, 27, 39, 151
homeostasis, 53, 151
hospitality, ix, 1,7, 16, 18, 20, 104, 151
human rights, xvi, 7, 11, 12, 21, 97, 114, 118, 119, 140, 141, 145, 151
humanitarian, 114, 116, 118, 120, 142, 151
humility, xvii, 151
Hutu, 105, 121, 151

identity, vii, 15, 16, 18, 20, 22, 28, 33, 36, 46, 55, 57, 61, 64, 68, 69, 79, 81, 84, 85, 88, 89, 94, 104, 106, 110, 120, 142, 145, 146, 151
Illich, Ivan, 39, 142, 144, 151
imagination, 5, 33, 37, 39, 41, 45,46, 57, 68, 151
in-group, 126, 151
Indian, 32, 33, 151
indifference, 55
Integral Ecology of Life, 7, 21
interdisciplinary, xii, 24, 29, 151
international community, 98, 99, 101, 151
interreligious peacebuilding, x, 103, 107, 111, 151
Israel, 2, 151

Jung, Carl, 39, 41, 42, 44, 45, 49, 68, 142, 145, 151

Kosovo, 86, 151

Laudato si, xvii, 144, 151
leadership, 21, 22, 71, 117, 123, 126, 131, 141, 145, 151
Lebanese, 22, 151
Lebanon, 27, 86, 151
Levi, Primo, 75, 151
Levinas, Emmanuel, 38, 44, 68, 143, 151
Lewin, Kurt, 83, 143, 151
liminal space, 38
locally led peacebuilding, 135, 151

Mali, 86, 151
Mary Hoch Center for Reconciliation, 130, 133, 151
mediation, 16, 55, 140, 151
mediator, 18, 60, 62, 109, 151
memory, 5, 12, 29, 30, 33, 45, 54, 60, 62, 65, 68, 70, 74, 75, 115, 151
Microcredit, 67, 151
microtraumas, 24
Middle East, 23, 60, 86, 151

migration, 15,16, 34
mindset, 15, 21, 25, 31, 33, 36, 41, 53, 73, 136, 151
Mirage, 56, 58, 60, 63, 66, 151
Miraggio, 5, 56
Mitchell, Christopher, 40, 122, 143, 144
mourning, 32, 151
myth, 17, 151

NGO, 126, 134, 136, 152

Ossetia, 33, 114–116, 140, 145, 152

pain, xv, ìxvi, 5, 13, 15, 25, 29, 30, 32, 34, 36, 40, 43, 44, 46, 47, 49, 51, 58, 66, 68, 70, 73, 84, 104, 117, 118, 125, 126, 152
Pakistani, 33, 152
Palestine, 60, 86, 152
paradigm, 20, 28, 39, 40, 135, 145, 152
peace, vii, x, xv, xvii, 3,4, 7, 11, 13, 17, 22, 23, 25, 27 31, 36, 61, 64, 70, 81, 87, 99, 100, 102, 105, 107, 109, 111, 113, 119, 121, 125, 127, 130, ì131, 133,.134, 136, 139, 145, 147, 148, 152, 153
person, ix, xv, xvii, 5, 7, 12, 14, 16, 19, 20, 23, 24, 27, 29, 31, 40, 43, 48, 55, 57, 62, 64, 66, 68, 70, 74, 80, 81, 84, 90, 98, 104, 116, 117, 119, 120
poisoned identity, 61
politics, xvi, 28, 143, 147, 152
Pope Francis, ix, xv, xvii, 3, 7, 104, 111, 144, 152
practice, vii, 2, 6, 11, 18, 21,22, 40, 44, 48, 51, 63, 82, 104, 113, 114, 118, 120, 125, 131, 140, 142, 144, 152
praxis, 4, 7, 145, 152
psycho-pedagogical, 11, 39, 152
psychological accommodation, 44, 45, 61, 152
psychological adjustment, 48, 49, 152
psychotherapy, 40, 131, 152
PTSD, 131, 132, 152

rationality, 2, 46, 55, 71, 74, 90, 152

reciprocity, 18, 24, 66, 152

reconciliation, 5, 12, 14, 36, 71, 72, 80, 103, 106, 108,109, 111, 126, 130, 133, 142, 152

relational bridge, 59, 65, 152

relational shock, 30, 43, 58, 60, 63, 131, 135, 152

relationship, ix, xii, 2, 4, 5, 16, 20, 23, 24, 27, 40, 43, 45, 47, 49, 51, 52, 56, 57, 59, 62, 63, 66, 68, 72, 90, 91, 109, 110, 115, 116, 124, 126, 136, 152

resilient, 2, 72, 152

responsibility, xvi, xvii, 28, 29, 31, 38, 145, 152

risk taking, 24, 152

Rondine d'Oro, 22

Rondine Method, iii, ix, xii, xvi, xvii, 1, 3, 7, 9, 11, 13, 18, 21, 23, 25, 27 28, 33, 35, 41, 43, 45, 47, 49, 51, 55, 59, 63, 67, 71, 74, 77, 81, 82, 97, 103, 105, 111, 113, 115, 117, 119, 121, 123, 125, 127, 129, 133, 136, 137, 152

Rondini, 15, 71, 84, 85

Rose Castle, 130, 132,133, 152

Rothbart, Daniel x, xii, 27, 104, 113,114, 116, 118, 120, 122, 124, 126, 127, 133, 145, 148, 152

Rublev, Andrei, 1, 2, 152

Russia, 115, 137, 140, 152

Rwanda, 121, 152

Sacks, Jonathan, 3, 145, 153

Saint Francis, xv, xvii, 153

scale, 21, 88, 91, 94, 120, 133, 135, 139, 142, 145, 146, 153

self-healing, 5, 153

Serbia, 16, 32, 86, 110 153

shock, 30, 43, 51, 58, 60, 63, 99, 131, 135, 152, 153

Sierra Leone, 22, 23, 71, 109, 153

social impact projects, 22, 153

stability, 18, 20, 28, 38, 45, 53, 54, 73, 74, 107, 163

stereotype, 43, 57, 135

stranger, 2, 3, 15, 61, 75, 153

subconscious, 36, 43, 44, 48, 54, 153

suffering, xv, 5, 12, 14, 16, 34, 36, 53, 58, 63, 65, 66, 69, 73, 74, 104, 105, 113, 114, 116, 119, 121, 123, 126, 153

Sullivan, Henry Stack, 40, 99, 141

sympathy, xvi, 104,

system, 53, 54, 82, 106, 114, 119, 127, 145, 153

theory, x, 4, 6, 19, 21, 31, 36, 39, 45, 63, 79,81, 103, 108, 111, 135, 140, 143, 145, 150, 153

therapy, 40, 41, 131, 142, 146, 153

Think Peace Learning Hub, 130, 133, 153

threat, vii, 16, 34, 51, 53, 105, 106, 145, 153

top down, 98, 101, 153

training, 11, 18, 20, 23, 27, 28, 34, 35, 39, 63, 71,72, 81, 87, 102, 117, 118, 121, 125, 127, 131, 132, 141, 143, 144, 153

transformation, x, xii, xvi, 3, 5, 11, 20,21, 25, 34, 37, 42, 46, 65, 67, 68, 103, 104, 106, 142, 149, 153

trauma, 5, 20, 24, 35, 36, 40, 43, 51, 53, 55, 63–65, 68, 73, 74, 104, 130, 133, 153

triggering events, 30, 153

trust, ix, xvi, xvii, 4, 5, 11, 13, 15, 17, 21, 23, 25, 28, 34, 36, 37, 39, 41–44, 52, 53, 55, 56, 59, 63, 67, 69, 71,73, 97, 99, 104, 106, 109, 153

Tutsi, 105, 153

Ulysses Path, 29, 70, 153

understanding, 4, 5, 28, 31, 40, 46, 49, 53, 61, 65, 72, 83, 90, 97, 99, 100, 102, 107, 109, 110, 115, 116, 119, 121, 126, 137, 153

United Nations, xvii, 71, 114, 118, 119, 153

Universal Declaration of Human Rights, xvi, 11, 119, 141
USAID, 99, 100, 153

Vaccari, Franco, 148, 154
vicious cycle, 51, 154
vision, xiii, xvi, 3, 16, 17, 23, 48, 53, 111, 115, 120, 154
vulnerability, 55, 104, 119, 141, 154
vulnerable, 4, 32, 113, ì114, 119, 154

war, vii, xii, xv, xvii, 2, 4, 6, 11, 18, 20, 25, 28, 30, 32, 35, 39, 43, 51, 52, 60, 64, 80, 85, 100, 102, 105, 115, 117, 119, 120, 137, 154

Weil, Simone, 39, 68, 135, 146, 154
Winnicott, Donald Woods, 39, 42, 49, 68, 135, 146, 154
witness, 16, 64, 154
World House, xii, 11, 13, 14, 17, 18, 20, 22, 25, 27, 29, 31, 35, 59, 66, 67, 71, 72, 84, 85, 87, 89, 91, 93, 95, 129, 137, 154
world language, 71
worldview, 53, 71, 73, 154

youth, xvii, 3, 19, 25, 109, 126, 143, 145, 154
Yunus, Muhammad, 67, 154

About the Contributors

Susan Allen is Associate Professor of Conflict Analysis and Resolution at the Jimmy and Rosalynn Carter School for Peace and Conflict Resolution at George Mason University in Fairfax, Virginia.

Anna Bertoni is a member of the Family Studies and Research University Centre of the Università Cattolica del Sacro Cuore of Milan (Italy).

Miguel H. Díaz holds the John Courtney Murray University Chair of Public Service at Loyola University Chicago and served as U.S. Ambassador to the Holy See from 2009 until 2012.

Alessandro Garuglieri, PTSTA-P psychologist and psychotherapist.

Charles Hauss is a veteran activist, author of eighteen books in comparative politics and peacebuilding, and Senior Fellow for Innovation at the Alliance for Peacebuilding.

Raffaella Iafrate is a member of the Family Studies and Research University Centre of the Università Cattolica del Sacro Cuore of Milan (Italy).

Michael David Kaiser is a professor at the Lutheran College Washington Semester program.

Ariela Pagani is a faculty member at the University of Urbino (University of Urbino Carlo Bo, Department of Humanities).

Gerard Powers is Director of Catholic Peace Studies at the Kroc Institute for International Peace Studies at the University of Notre Dame in South Bend, Indiana.

Daniel Rothbart is Professor of Conflict Analysis and Resolution at the Jimmy and Rosalynn Carter School for Peace and Conflict Resolution at George Mason University in Fairfax, Virginia.

Franco Vaccari is an Italian psychologist, academic, and activist and the founder and president of Rondine Cittadella della Pace. Married with two children, he graduated in psychology from La Sapienza University in Rome. He works as a freelance psychologist. He is the founder and director of the New Psychology Laboratory, a center for research and action in the psychological and pedagogical field. Vaccari is the author of numerous educational and scientific publications as well as a columnist for several Italian newspapers. He has held numerous academic lectures and seminars at Italian and international universities, mainly in the United States, Canada, and the South Caucasus.

www.ingramcontent.com/pod-product-compliance
Lightning Source LLC
Chambersburg PA
CBHW031137270326
41929CB00011B/1655